United States General Accounting Office

GAO

Report to the Honorable Norman Y. Mineta, Secretary of Transportation, and the Honorable Donald H. Rumsfeld, Secretary of Defense

January 2002

AVIATION SAFETY

FAA and DOD Response to Similar Safety Concerns

I0438991

GAO

Accountability ★ Integrity ★ Reliability

GAO-02-77

Contents

Abbreviations

AD	Airworthiness Directive
AMCOM	Aviation and Missile Command
ATSRAC	Aging Transport Systems Rulemaking Advisory Committee
AWIGG	Aircraft Wiring and Inert Gas Generator Working Group
CPDF	Central Personnel Data File
DOD	Department of Defense
DODIG	Department of Defense Office of Inspector General
DOJ	Department of Justice
DOT	Department of Transportation
DOTIG	Department of Transportation Office of Inspector General
DSB	Defense Science Board
EAPAS	Enhanced Airworthiness Program for Airplane Systems
EGPWS	Enhanced Ground Proximity Warning System
FAA	Federal Aviation Administration
FOQA	Flight Operational Quality Assurance
FSCAP	Flight Safety Critical Aircraft Parts
GAIN	Global Aviation Information Network
GAO	General Accounting Office
GIDEP	Government-Industry Data Exchange Program
GPWS	Ground Proximity Warning System
IRT	Independent Review Team
JSSC	Joint Service Safety Chiefs
MOA	Memorandum of Agreement
NTSB	National Transportation Safety Board
OC-ALC	Oklahoma City Air Logistics Command
OPM	Office of Personnel Management
OSD	Office of the Secretary of Defense
OSHA	Occupational Health and Safety Act
SAE	Society of Automotive Engineers
SWAMP	Severe Wind And Moisture-Prone
TAWS	Terrain Awareness Warning System
TCAS	Traffic Alert and Collision Avoidance System
TKT	Teflon-Kapton-Teflon
UPN	Unapproved Parts Notification

United States General Accounting Office
Washington, DC 20548

January 22, 2002

The Honorable Norman Y. Mineta
Secretary of Transportation

The Honorable Donald H. Rumsfeld
Secretary of Defense

Safety of aircraft is a paramount concern in both civilian and military aviation because safety deficiencies can cost lives and equipment and affect mission accomplishment. The Federal Aviation Administration (FAA) and the military services often face common safety issues as they oversee the operation of similar aircraft or even dissimilar aircraft that use common parts and materials. Our preliminary work, however, showed that in some cases FAA and the military services have taken different actions to address similar aviation safety concerns. We recognize that there could be reasonable explanations for FAA and the military services taking different approaches in addressing such concerns.

To shed more light in this area, we used a case study approach supplemented by a review of FAA's and Department of Defense's (DOD) aviation safety oversight processes and related interdepartmental communication efforts to (1) examine different responses by FAA and DOD/military services to similar aviation safety concerns and (2) assess the processes used by FAA and DOD[1] to communicate information about similar aviation safety concerns. To select case studies for this review, we identified aviation safety problems shared by FAA and the military services, selected examples in which FAA and DOD/military services had taken a different approach to solving a similar aviation safety problem or had a need to be informed about such a problem, and discussed potential case studies with FAA and the military services.

To examine different responses by FAA and the military services, we used two cases in which FAA and the military services took different actions or

---

[1]For the balance of the report we refer to FAA and the military services, rather than FAA and DOD. We recognize that DOD has ultimate authority for directing the services' actions on aviation safety oversight. Also, unless otherwise noted, the Coast Guard, which is a part of Department of Transportation (DOT), is included under the discussions of the military services. Despite its peacetime missions, the Coast Guard's aviation safety oversight activities parallel those of the military services.

similar actions at a different pace when faced with common aviation safety problems. These cases pertain to aircraft wiring insulation and cockpit equipment designed to improve safety and support quality assurance programs for flight operations. In addition, we selected two case studies to assess the exchange of aviation safety information between FAA and the military services. These include a specific brand of wire rope used in the construction of aircraft control cables and problems of fuel pump performance and overheating in fuel tanks in the E-4B, a military variant of the Boeing 747.

We interviewed and obtained relevant documentation from federal officials and others familiar with FAA's and the military services' aviation safety oversight systems. We asked these officials about the extent to which these entities share information on aviation safety issues of common interest. This review focuses primarily on issues involving similar civilian and military aircraft equipment, parts, and material issues related to aviation safety, rather than issues concerning the operation of aircraft. It does not address aviation security issues, such as hijacking, sabotage, or terrorist activities. See appendix I for additional details on our scope and methodology.

Results in Brief

For one of the two cases that we reviewed where FAA and the military services reacted differently to similar aviation safety concerns, the differences reflect the agency's and services' different missions and operational environments. In the second case, the military services have reacted more slowly than civil aviation due to resource tradeoffs between aviation safety and other mission-readiness issues.

In the first case, when the Navy identified potential safety problems concerning the use of a specific type of wire insulation on aircraft in a moist operating environment, each of the military services and FAA assessed the insulation's safety in various environments and responded differently. For example, FAA issued advisory notifications to the civil aviation community to help identify and minimize the potential risks associated with the use of this insulation; the Navy promptly removed it from areas prone to infiltration by moisture; while the Coast Guard lagged behind the Navy in removing this insulation, it later took the most extensive action by systematically removing it from an entire fleet of helicopters after it experienced in-flight fires. These different responses are largely a function of these entities' respective missions and operational environments. In the second case, the military services have lagged as much as two decades behind FAA in requiring the installation of collision avoidance technologies aboard passenger-carrying aircraft. Despite the attention focused on the need to equip such aircraft with safety alerting systems[2] after the 1996 crash involving the death of then-Secretary of Commerce Ronald Brown, timelines for equipping such aircraft extend out as far as 2009. The installation of these devices must compete with other demands to ensure mission readiness. Some DOD officials expressed concern that aviation safety does not receive adequate visibility. The office responsible for aviation safety currently occupies a relatively low organizational position within the Office of the Secretary of Defense (OSD). As a result of downsizing by OSD several years ago, five safety positions, which shared responsibility for aviation safety issues, were abolished and a single staff member hired. This staff member's responsibilities include aviation safety and a number of other responsibilities, including compliance with the Occupational Safety and Health Act of 1970 (OSHA), as amended; fire and emergency services; range and weapons safety; and traffic transportation.

For the two cases where we evaluated the communication processes between FAA and the military services, our review showed that existing formal networks of communication have not always been sufficient to ensure the comprehensive exchange of all critical aviation safety information. Specifically, we found (1) a lack of a common definition of what constitutes an aviation safety hazard of mutual concern and (2) gaps in the formal communication processes, which caused delays in bringing critical safety information to the attention of key officials. In addition, the informal information exchange is currently sustained largely by personal rather than formal agency/service relationships, and is therefore vulnerable to the retirement of key aviation safety personnel and senior leaders. For these reasons, we are making a recommendation to improve the formal processes used by FAA and the military services to exchange aviation safety information of mutual interest.

Background

FAA, an agency located within DOT is responsible for regulating and promoting the safety of civil aviation. The Coast Guard is part of DOT, except when operating as a service in the Navy during time of declared

---

[2]Traffic Alert and Collision Avoidance Systems (TCAS) alert pilots to potential collisions with other airborne aircraft, and Ground Proximity Warning Systems (GPWS) alert pilots to impending collisions with terrain.

war or when the president otherwise directs;[3] however, the Coast Guard follows its own rules for aviation safety oversight, which parallel the structure and operations followed by the military services rather than those of FAA.

In contrast to FAA, DOD is both an operator and a regulator of aviation for the military services. Its primary mission is national defense, one component of which is aviation safety. OSD maintains oversight of the military services' aircraft aviation safety processes but has delegated to the heads of the military departments the responsibility for aviation safety programs. For example, the secretary's office is responsible for issuing policies and directives pertaining to aviation safety that the military services must implement as they address their respective missions. Within OSD, aviation safety is the responsibility of the Office of Safety and Occupational Health, under the Office of the Deputy Undersecretary for Installations and Environment, which, among other responsibilities, includes traffic safety, OSHA compliance, and toxic hazards.

There are three key similarities and three differences between the aviation safety oversight systems used by FAA and the military services. They share common internal processes for disseminating safety information; managing aviation safety risks (e.g., they each use variations of a five-step process); and certifying that aircraft meet civil aviation standards (FAA provides the certification services to the military at no cost). They differ, however, in their processes to certify that aircraft meet their unique safety standards and to investigate aircraft accidents, as well as in the timetables and thresholds for acting on potential and identified aviation safety problems. For example, the command and control structure of the military services allows immediate action to be ordered, such as the grounding of a fleet of aircraft, after weighing the impact on their respective missions. In contrast, although FAA can and has taken similar immediate action when necessary, the agency often has more to consider before taking equivalent action, such as consulting with airlines and other stakeholders, given the potential ramifications for the nation's economy and the public interest. See appendix III for additional information on key similarities and differences between FAA's and the military services' aviation safety oversight systems.

---

[3]The Coast Guard normally performs multiple civil missions, such as maritime search and rescue, law enforcement, and environmental protection. During wartime, the Coast Guard operates under the authority of the Department of the Navy.

Flight operations for military aircraft can differ from those of civil aircraft in their nature and severity (e.g., turns may be made at steeper angles and aircraft may ascend and descend at higher speeds). Although standard parts may be common, the stress on the parts and materials in the environment in which they are used may be quite different. As such, the Coast Guard and the Navy frequently fly aircraft in close proximity to water,[4] a condition that poses special maintenance concerns, while most commercial civil aircraft are not typically exposed to similar conditions. In addition, according to some military officials, military aircraft can be operated closer to the "edge of the envelope"—maximum recommended speeds, weight, and other parameters—than commercial civil aircraft. Such conditions can also accelerate wear of aircraft.

FAA and the military services oversee the safety of some similar aircraft types,[5] such as the Boeing 737 and executive jet aircraft. See appendix II for a more detailed listing. Even dissimilar civil and military aircraft often have common parts and materials such as bolts, fasteners, and wiring. Civil and military aircraft are manufactured, modified, and repaired using standard type parts, although their application may differ. Interdepartmental communication about aviation safety issues of mutual interest is important to (1) ensure timely correction of structural, mechanical, or material weaknesses on aircraft that could lead to safety problems (e.g., loss of lives and aircraft) and (2) make effective use of federal dollars by sharing lessons learned about specific problems.

Actions of FAA and the Military Services to Address Similar Aviation Safety Concerns Vary

Similar aviation safety concerns do not necessarily lead FAA and the military services to take the same actions to mitigate or eliminate them or to act at the same pace. Different actions taken by these entities based on assessments of safety risk can in some cases be appropriate and reflect mission differences or, in other cases, may not seem warranted. The examples below, describing the potential safety concerns associated with the choice of electrical wire insulation and the pace of equipping aircraft

---

[4]Both the Navy and Coast Guard fly their aircraft in close proximity to water, often for extended periods of time, which can corrode aircraft. For example, Coast Guard helicopters take on water from rescue swimmer training and rescue operations and are often not protected from moist conditions due to a lack of adequate hangar space.

[5]For purposes of this report, "similar aircraft" refers to aircraft types that civilian and military entities operate, such as the Boeing 737, 747, and DC 10. In some cases the military versions have been modified.

with warning devices to alert pilots to impending collisions, illustrates this point.

Assessments of Similar Aviation Safety Risks by FAA and the Military Services Can Vary

Given different operating environments, the same safety risk can vary in probability and/or severity. For example, one of the military services could determine that, based on its mission requirements and a unique and harsh operating environment, an aviation safety hazard poses an extremely high risk because it is likely to occur frequently and have a critical or catastrophic impact. Conversely, FAA might determine that, based on the standard operating environment for civil aviation, the hazard poses a low safety risk because it is unlikely to occur, even if its severity is deemed critical. Given the prohibitively high cost of eliminating all potential aviation safety hazards, officials responsible for aviation safety must often accept some level of residual risk. FAA and military service officials acknowledged that some of the components used in preparing such safety risk estimates are subjective, but said they rely to the extent practical on technical experts to inform the decision-making process.

FAA and the Military Services Took Different Actions to Address Potential Safety Concerns Posed by a Type of Wire Insulation

When faced with a similar potential safety concern posed by the use of a specific type of wire insulation known as aromatic polyimide, FAA and each of the military services used common research findings, evidence collected from flight operations, and mission priorities to independently assess the safety risk of continued use of this wire insulation. Each arrived at different decisions about the level of hazard it posed and the actions warranted based largely upon mission differences and specific design requirements. Aviation safety officials involved in these risk assessments provided some explanations for the differing results.

- Environment: One of the main considerations used to assess its safety risk was the operating environment of the aircraft. For example, FAA also considered that naval aircraft routinely operate in more harsh environments than commercial aircraft–on aircraft carriers where they are constantly exposed to moisture.
- Ballistic Testing: To explain differences between FAA's decision and the Navy's decision, some officials pointed out that the genesis of the Navy's concerns grew out of ballistic testing– a survivability issue that was not a concern for FAA and commercial operators. For example, in 1986, Navy tests found that bullets fired into an aircraft could sever wires, cause arc tracking events, and trip circuit breakers.
- Aircraft Design Dictates Wire Installation Practices: According to FAA and military safety officials, another consideration that guided FAA to a

different result from the Navy is that transport passenger aircraft have much more room to run wires than fighter aircraft. As a result, wires require much less bending that can potentially cause their insulation to degrade.

The Navy took the lead in identifying and examining potential problems associated with the use of this wire insulation type and in mitigating hazards. In the mid-1980s, when the Navy began experiencing problems with this wire insulation, it enlisted the support of experts from other military services and FAA to further characterize the problems and identify possible solutions. Researchers determined that prolonged exposure of this type of wire insulation to moisture could cause it to deteriorate and that it was susceptible to arc tracking. Arc tracking can occur when two cracks in the insulation are close enough together to allow the current to form a conductive path between them at temperatures that can cause the insulation to char and carbonize. This carbonization can turn the insulation into an electrical conductor, and, eventually, can trip a circuit breaker. When a pilot presses the switch to reset a tripped circuit breaker, an entire wire bundle can be disabled and potentially compromise the safety of an aircraft's entire electrical system.

Ultimately, the Navy and the Coast Guard took the most active measures to address potential problems with aromatic polyimide, which some experts attribute to these entities' unique aircraft operations near water. In December 1985, the Navy decided that aromatic polyimide would no longer be its wiring insulator of choice and subsequently removed it selectively from parts of aircraft where it was most problematic (e.g., fore and aft flaps, wheel wells, and around unsecured seals that could leak). The Coast Guard lagged behind the Navy in taking action to address problems with this wire insulation; however, it took the most extensive action by stripping it from its largest fleet of helicopters as a precautionary measure after occurrences of in-flight fires and cockpit smoke and fumes between 1993 and 1996. While no aircraft were destroyed, these incidents led to poor visibility in the cockpit and, in some cases, the loss of all electrically powered flight instruments. A senior Coast Guard safety official said that the Coast Guard completed removal of this wire insulation from its entire fleet of H-65 helicopters in September 2001. In contrast, the Army did not experience similar safety problems. While it independently confirmed the Navy's findings in 1986, the Army concluded that it did not have the same problems with aromatic polyimide. The Army did have durability concerns, however; it found the degree to which aromatic polyimide chafes in Apache and Blackhawk helicopters is unacceptable over time and decided to remove it gradually as it refurbished older aircraft.

In response to the Navy's finding of potential hazards with the use of aromatic polyimide, FAA conducted independent research, tracked related research and operational data from industry and the military services, and decided that mandating the removal of this wire insulation from commercial aircraft was not warranted. However, FAA did issue three Advisory Circulars related to the use of this wire insulation type, in 1987, 1991, and 1998, to provide policy guidance to help prevent electrical problems and potential fires and to describe acceptable practices for aircraft inspection and repair, including wire installation.

Recognizing the need for sustained attention to aircraft wiring issues, FAA has ongoing efforts to assess the health of wire in aging aircraft through its Aging Transport Systems Rulemaking Advisory Committee (ATSRAC). To date, working groups under ATSRAC have conducted visual (nonintrusive) and extensive physical (intrusive) inspections of wiring on aging aircraft. However, according to National Transportation Safety Board (NTSB) officials, it is too soon to determine how well the agency is doing in its assessment. These officials pointed out that ATSRAC has a seven-step objective of reviewing wiring in aging aircraft, and its recent intrusive inspection is only one step in the process.

In August 2001, FAA announced a new initiative, the Enhanced Airworthiness Program for Airplane Systems (EAPAS), a cooperative effort with industry that is intended to (1) enhance the safety of aircraft wiring from design and installation through retirement, (2) increase awareness of wiring degradation, (3) implement better procedures for wiring maintenance and design, and (4) ensure that the aviation community is informed. In the same month, the Transportation Safety Board of Canada announced that, as a result of its investigation of the crash of Swissair Flight 111, it (1) concluded wire failure can play an active role in fire initiation and (2) recommended a more stringent certification test regime. FAA officials told us that the agency has not yet responded to the conclusions and recommendations of the Transportation Safety Board of Canada. See appendix IV for a more detailed summary of actions taken by FAA and the military services to address concerns about aromatic polyimide.

The Military Services Acted More Slowly Than FAA to Require Installation of Cockpit Safety Equipment to Reduce Crashes Into Terrain, and Midair Collisions, and to Monitor Other Potential Safety Problems

The military services have lagged as much as two decades behind FAA in requiring the installation of cockpit technology in passenger-carrying aircraft to alert pilots to impending collisions. In 1974, FAA responded to NTSB recommendations by requiring operators of large commercial aircraft to equip the cockpits of these aircraft with Ground Proximity Warning Systems (GPWS) to provide pilots with warnings of potential collisions with terrain (land or water). FAA extended this GPWS requirement to operators of smaller airplanes and turbojet-powered airplanes with 10 or more passenger seats in 1978. However, the military services did not plan to systematically install GPWS in passenger- and troop-carrying aircraft until after the 1996 crash of a military aircraft carrying then-Secretary of Commerce Ronald Brown and 34 others. Subsequently, a senior military safety official reported that the crash would almost certainly have been prevented had the aircraft been equipped with enhanced GPWS. The enhanced version of GPWS provides flight crews with earlier auditory and visual warnings of terrain, forward-looking capability, and more time to make smoother and more gradual corrective actions.

FAA also took action in 1989—based on a 1987 congressional mandate—to reduce the number of midair collisions by requiring certain civil aircraft to be equipped with Traffic Alert and Collision Avoidance Systems (TCAS). These systems help pilots to avoid midair collisions by providing them with messages of an impending collision with another aircraft. According to FAA, since the advanced version of TCAS (TCAS II) was introduced in 1993, civil midair collisions in the United States have declined by 80 percent. While acknowledging the benefits of TCAS, the military services have equipped their passenger-carrying aircraft with TCAS at a slower pace. For example, in August 1996, the Air Force published its Navigation and Safety Equipment Master Plan for DOD Passenger-Carrying Aircraft, which established guidance for equipping passenger- and troop-carrying aircraft, including GPWS and TCAS in two implementation phases. Phase 1 requires installation by 2001 of all equipment used to transport senior military leaders, and Phase 2 requires installation of this equipment on remaining passenger- and troop-carrying aircraft by 2005. As of January 2001, the Air Force had equipped 49 percent of its passenger- and troop-carrying fleet with these technologies, but in some cases the timelines for equipping these aircraft with GPWS and TCAS extend out as far as 2009. As of July 2001, the Navy had equipped less than 20 percent of its passenger-carrying fleet with GPWS[6] and TCAS. According to an official from the Department of the Army, as of August 2001, units had equipped 38 of the Army's 294 fixed wing aircraft with enhanced GPWS and 90 of these same aircraft with TCAS. The remaining fixed wing aircraft must be equipped with these technologies by fiscal year 2006. The Army has not equipped any of its rotary wing aircraft (i.e., helicopters) with GPWS or TCAS and currently has no plans to do so. In contrast, by 1998, the Coast Guard had installed TCAS in all of its fixed wing and rotary wing aircraft. In addition, according to a senior Coast Guard safety official, it has equipped its C-130 fleet with GPWS, and the majority of the remainder of its fleet is helicopters; however, due to the erratic nature of rotorcraft flight as compared to fixed wing aircraft flight,[7] making use of GPWS on helicopters is much more difficult and the technology development lags behind that for fixed wing aircraft. This official stressed that as such there is no FAA mandate that civil helicopters be equipped with GPWS or its enhanced version. See appendix V for more details on GPWS and TCAS.

In addition, some major U.S. air carriers, in coordination with FAA, have generally acted sooner than the military services to install passenger-carrying aircraft with flight data recorders and to establish programs that collect and analyze aircraft data from routine passenger flights to detect potential safety, training, and maintenance problems. These programs are commonly referred to as Flight Operational Quality Assurance (FOQA) programs. In July 1995, as part of FAA's strategy to achieve significant reductions in aviation accident rates, the agency initiated a 3-year, $5.5 million FOQA Demonstration Project to promote the voluntary implementation of FOQA programs by U.S. airlines. In response, several major carriers have initiated FOQA programs.

In October 1999, the safety chiefs for each of the military services agreed that FOQA had value and endorsed projects and research by all services. A Memorandum of Agreement signed by the services' safety chiefs in August 2000 followed this. Efforts by the military services to initiate FOQA programs are in the very early stages, with the Air Force taking the lead through a demonstration project using the C-17 aircraft. The Air Force

---

[6] The Navy is currently installing GPWS and plans to install the enhanced version sometime in the future.

[7] Helicopters can stop, pedal turn, and hover, while fixed wing aircraft are often operated in a fairly narrow band of forward motion, which makes their near-term flight path more predictable.

selected a software contractor for its FOQA program in June 2001 and has since begun analyzing data it has collected since 1994 from nearly 11,000 flights. See appendix VI for additional information.

Some officials with OSD told us that because of the relatively low organizational position of aviation safety within DOD this issue does not receive the visibility that is warranted. Aviation safety is located within the office of the Deputy Undersecretary of Defense for Installations and Environment within the Office of Safety and Occupational Health and is one of 26 competing oversight responsibilities of this office, which includes OSHA compliance, traffic safety, and toxic hazards. Currently there is no aviation safety manager/officer for OSD. Several years ago, five safety positions were abolished as part of an OSD downsizing effort and a single staff member was hired to cover aviation safety and a multitude of other responsibilities including OSHA compliance, fire and emergency services, and range, weapons, traffic, and transportation safety.

Shortcomings in Existing Processes Used for Sharing Aviation Safety Information

While FAA and the military services have numerous mechanisms in place to exchange aviation safety information, we found (1) a lack of a common definition of what constitutes aviation safety information of mutual concern and (2) gaps in the formal processes currently used to exchange aviation safety information. These gaps are illustrated by two cases where existing formal networks of communication were not sufficient to ensure prompt and comprehensive exchanges of aviation safety information and follow-up actions responding to identified problems. The heavy reliance by FAA and the military services on informal communication networks to exchange aviation safety information is vulnerable to an expected wave of retirements.

Numerous Mechanisms Are Used to Exchange Aviation Safety Information

FAA and the military services have established numerous mechanisms for exchanging aviation safety information, including informal networks among aviation safety personnel, use of Web sites, meetings among senior leaders and attending each others' meetings and conferences.

- Informal Networks: Technical staff at FAA and the military services (e.g., aerospace engineers) have developed an informal network that has facilitated the exchange of information about similar aviation safety issues. These officials reported that they have set some joint research priorities, routinely share research findings and information gleaned from accident investigations, and conduct joint aircraft testing. According to FAA and DOD officials in the research and development arena, the exchange of information on aviation safety is excellent, routine, and reliable. This communication has provided them with a means of alerting colleagues in other agencies and services about key issues or problems. These officials cautioned that the effectiveness of this type of communication is attributable to its informal nature and that formalizing these processes would hinder rather than help their work.

For example, officials from the FAA Technical Center, military services, and National Aeronautics and Space Administration meet at least semiannually to set common research priorities, share the research workload, and, in some cases, this has led to formal cost-sharing for research and development on aging aircraft systems. This allows each of these entities to leverage the federal dollars spent on common aviation safety problems. While formal initiatives are in place regarding shared federal agency research on aviation safety and aging aircraft systems, these meetings and research sharing activities evolved from informal communication. One outgrowth of this informal communication has been the sharing of costs by the Navy and FAA to develop a new "smart" circuit breaker that can detect and interrupt electrical surges associated with arc tracking and minimize the damage to wires. This technology should help to prevent much of the damage that currently occurs and goes undetected. In addition, miniaturizing this new circuit breaker is a priority for both the military services and FAA, for example, for use on military aircraft that have limited space and aboard civil aircraft to increase the number of functions for which the circuit breaker can be used. Such sharing of aviation safety research priorities helps to ensure the timely exchange of lessons learned among FAA and the military services (e.g., about how a specific aviation safety hazard was addressed) and the effective use of federal funds dedicated to aviation safety oversight.

- Use of Web Sites: Exchanges of information between FAA and the military services also take place when information of mutual interest is posted to their respective Web sites. For example, the Air Force currently maintains the most exhaustive database on the hazards of aircraft striking birds. It is used extensively by the other military services and FAA to identify, among other things, altitudes and migratory flight paths commonly used by bird species. It also serves as a mechanism to alert pilots and aviation safety officials to avoid certain flight levels and airspace, when practical. In addition, the Army's Aviation and Missile Command (AMCOM) makes use of its Web site to post critical aviation safety messages (stripped of privileged and classified information) pertaining to its helicopter fleet, thus allowing the other military services and FAA to monitor potential safety hazards. Similarly, FAA's Web site provides access to many of the agency's safety databases as well as airworthiness directives, which are generally posted on a real-time basis.

- Communication Among FAA and DOD Senior Leaders: Senior leaders at FAA and DOD reported that they generally keep informed about aviation safety issues common to both organizations through networking, such as telephone and working lunches. According to a senior DOD official, this networking has been a very effective way to exchange information with FAA, as senior leaders from both entities have become well acquainted and use these personal relationships to keep lines of communication open and active. A senior FAA safety official also characterized informal working relations between FAA and DOD as effective.

- Other Mechanisms for Information Exchange: FAA and the military services use a range of other mechanisms for exchanging information about aviation safety. These include attending each other's meetings and professional conferences, exchanging practices for assessing safety risks, and developing technical standards. Table 1 provides further examples of ways that FAA and the military services communicate.

Table 1: Examples of Mechanisms for Information Exchange Between FAA and the Military Services

Communication mechanism	Information exchange activities
Commercial Aviation Safety Team	This team was created to identify, analyze, and prioritize aviation safety hazards and appropriate actions to mitigate these problems.
Government-Industry Data Exchange Program (GIDEP)	A cooperative activity between industry and government managed by the Navy through an agreement of the Joint Logistics Commanders. Provides a medium to exchange technical information about the quality and reliability of parts, components, equipment, and services used by the federal government. It is not aviation-specific.
Aging Transport Systems Rulemaking Advisory Committee (ATSRAC)	Currently, FAA, industry, DOD, and other stakeholders are conducting research on wiring systems in aging aircraft.
Military Flight Operational Quality Assurance (FOQA) conferences	Two such conferences have been held to share information among the airlines and the military services on the FOQA concept and its implementation.
Safety Risk Management Conferences	FAA and NASA sponsor an annual conference on Risk Analysis and Safety Performance Measurement. These conferences have been attended by the military services.
Society of Automotive Engineers (SAE)	A subset of this group is developing specifications for the new "smart" circuit breaker. Two engineers, one from the Naval Air Systems Command and the other from FAA's Technical Center, are leading this effort.
Global Aviation Information Network (GAIN)	This network is still in the early stages of development. Ultimately, it will provide a means to voluntarily exchange information among users worldwide, including the military, to improve aviation safety.
Meetings Among Senior Leaders	Senior DOD and FAA leaders invite their counterparts to attend aviation safety meetings (e.g., FAA is a permanent guest of the Joint Service Safety Chiefs and a participant in the Joint Aeronautical Commanders Group).
Aviation Rulemaking Advisory Committee	A formal FAA advisory committee established in 1991. It is comprised of representatives from the aviation community and provides the agency with industry input during FAA's rulemaking activities. DOD is not a standing member, but participates on occasion.
Memorandums of Understanding/Memorandums of Agreement	These memorandums are used to clarify how DOT/FAA and DOD work together (e.g., the sharing of civil and military airspace and information on air carriers' performance).
DOD liaisons at FAA	DOD liaisons working at FAA focus primarily on air traffic control issues; however, they relay requests for safety information to appropriate officials when requested.
Risk Management Information System (RMIS)	Software designed by the Army to collect and share information internally, with the other services, and agencies on a near real-time basis.
Flight Safety Critical Aircraft Parts (FSCAP) Project	A joint DOD and FAA effort to identify, dispose of, and control military surplus FSCAP available for civil purchase.
Interagency agreement regarding information exchange about problem parts and materials	Agreement signed in 1997 by FAA, DOT Office of Inspector General, Federal Bureau of Investigation, U.S. Customs and Defense Criminal Investigative Service regarding the exchange of information and technical support for suspect aviation parts.

Source: FAA and the military services.

FAA and the Military Services Have Not Developed a Common Definition of Aviation Safety Information of Mutual Concern

FAA and the military services have not developed a common definition of aviation safety information of mutual interest, and, in particular, what information should be considered critical. As a result, the information exchanged is based on individual judgment rather than on the systematic identification and exchange of information. Various definitions of critical aviation safety information have been established, such as that used by DOD for procuring aircraft materials and parts.[8] Policies have also been established to facilitate the exchange of aviation safety information of common interest between FAA and the military services; however, the basis for such communication is unclear and left up to individuals' interpretation. A fundamental step in developing this definition is establishing the universe of civil aircraft and their military aircraft derivatives, something senior FAA officials told us the agency has not been able to do.[9] See appendix II. Such a definition is needed to help ensure that all aviation safety information of common interest, especially that deemed critical, is promptly identified and reported to responsible officials.

Gaps Exist in the Processes Used By FAA and the Military Services to Exchange Aviation Safety Information of Mutual Concern

While FAA and the military services routinely exchange some aviation safety information of mutual concern, there are gaps in the processes used by both entities, including the sharing of how specific aviation safety concerns were addressed. For example, FAA sends its emergency Airworthiness Directives (AD)—a type of critical safety information—to only five U.S. military addressees, as requested by the military services, with the same level of urgency that they are sent to owners and operators

---

[8]The Department of Defense Standard Practice for System Safety defines safety critical as "a term applied to any condition, event, operation, process or item whose proper recognition, control, performance, or tolerance is essential to safety system operation and support (e.g., safety critical function). MIL-STD-882D (Feb. 10, 2000).

[9]Both FAA and the military services also rely on airframe manufacturers to collect and maintain data on potential aviation safety risks on similar civil and military aircraft and common parts and materials.

of civil aircraft.[10,11] These military addressees represent only a small subset of the military entities that could be affected.[12] FAA officials told us that it has added specific military users to its list of addressees, but has had limited success maintaining accurate and current contact information.

Despite FAA's general practice of posting emergency ADs to its Web site in real time, the site contains a disclaimer that the agency cannot guarantee the accuracy of the information it posts—for instance, the information posted could be vulnerable to tampering from computer viruses[13] or computer hackers. As a result, FAA requires that all emergency ADs be sent immediately via telegram or fax to owners and operators of civil aircraft and that their receipt be documented. While FAA is not required to send these directives to the military services,[14] it appears prudent to do so when it involves information of mutual interest, given their common responsibilities for aviation safety oversight.

Similarly, the military services provide FAA with some of their aviation safety information, but generally not with the same level of urgency with which they distribute it to the other services. For example, the Army's Aviation and Missile Command strips privileged and classified information from its critical safety messages pertaining to its helicopter fleet, sends them all to the other military services and FAA, and posts them to its Web site. In contrast, the Navy uses its judgment to send some of its aviation safety messages to FAA, while the Air Force's, Coast Guard's, and Army's

---

[10]FAA officials said that the agency's distribution of ADs relies on the FAA Civil Aircraft Registry and Civil Operations databases. For DOD aircraft, FAA distributes ADs according to DOD's requests. It is FAA's understanding that DOD wants ADs sent to certain specific contact offices, not to the operating units.

[11]Army officials said that AMCOM receives and reviews all emergency ADs from FAA and, when necessary, converts them into Safety of Flight and Aviation Safety Action Messages. They further noted that this centralized control is necessary to ensure compliance and because they do not want such FAA notices going to units that are not affected by a given message.

[12]As of July 18, 2001, FAA's addressee list for emergency ADs included five U.S. military recipients as follows: Naval Air Systems Command, Jacksonville, Florida (TPE331 engine); U.S. Army Aviation and Troop Command, St. Louis, Missouri (BHT-206 engine); U.S. Air Force, Scott Air Force Base (DC-9 and JT8D engine); U.S. Air Force, Oklahoma City, Oklahoma (Boeing-737-700); and U.S. Navy, Pentagon (DC-8 and DC-9).

[13]Access to FAA's Web site was disrupted in August 2001 by a computer virus.

[14]FAA is responsible for notifying owners and operators of aircraft on the agency's civil aircraft registry of airworthiness directives. Military aircraft are not listed in this directory.

Safety Centers generally provide aviation safety information to FAA only upon request.

The formal processes used by FAA and the military services to exchange aviation safety information of mutual concern, including information critical to flight safety, have not always been sufficient to ensure the comprehensive exchange of such information. While informal communication networks have helped to facilitate the exchange of aviation safety information, these exchanges are not required and systematic, and do not provide assurances that such information is exchanged in a timely manner. The automatic exchange of critical safety information is important to the safe operation of both civil and military aviation to help ensure that entities that could be affected receive notification promptly to provide them with as much time as possible to mitigate or eliminate a given hazard and avoid potential loss of lives and aircraft.

Two Cases Illustrate How FAA and the Military Services Do Not Always Exchange Critical Aviation Safety Information on a Systematic and Timely Basis

The importance of effective and timely information sharing between civil and military aviation entities on aviation safety issues was highlighted during the investigation of the 1996 crash of TWA Flight 800. It was not discovered until 1999 that the Air Force had contracted with Boeing in the late 1970s to study problems it experienced with fuel pumps and overheating in the center fuel tanks in the E-4B aircraft—the military variant of the Boeing 747. The Air Force was concerned about the E-4B engines continuing to run satisfactorily if a main (wing) fuel tank pump malfunctioned. There was also a concern over running of the air conditioning packs under the center wing fuel tank for extended periods of time (e.g., for 48 hours when operated in an alert mode). In this mode, the center wing tank was full of fuel, and heated up slowly to a high temperature. Boeing found that, under certain circumstances, air conditioning wires running through the fuel tank could create a potential safety problem, but determined that the engine would continue to operate successfully provided certain operating restrictions were implemented. While the central focus of the Air Force's concerns and Boeing's analysis was fuel pump performance, not fuel vapor flammability, NTSB officials said that the information contained in this report would have assisted them with their investigations of fuel tank overheating.

A senior NTSB official told us that it is not likely that earlier sharing of the report's findings would have prevented the crash of TWA Flight 800. However, had NTSB received the study in 1996 following the crash, valuable time and resources in conducting its investigation could have been saved. In August 2000, NTSB released its report on the TWA Flight 800 accident, which included the following statement regarding the report Boeing prepared for the Air Force on fuel tank overheating in the E4-B:

The Safety Board recognizes that the military variant of the 747 is not directly comparable to the civilian 747 and that the focus of that study was fuel pump functionality, not flammability. Nonetheless, it is unfortunate that potentially relevant information about 747 center wing [fuel] tank overheating and corrective measures were not provided to the FAA or to 747 operators earlier.

In addition, according to the NTSB chairman and director of aviation safety, the report might have been helpful to NTSB in its investigation of a Boeing 737 aircraft explosion in 1990 at Manila Airport in the Philippines. The explosion occurred in the aircraft's center fuel tank. Both the chairman and the director said that it is possible that if they had received this study in 1990, safety recommendations made as a result of the TWA Flight 800 investigation concerning fuel tanks might have been issued sooner. See appendix VII for more information about this case.

According to DOD, the wire rope produced by Strandflex and used to construct aircraft control cables is critical to the safe operation of flight control systems, such as aircraft rudders, steering, and brakes, on affected aircraft, while FAA officials contend that it is not always critical to flight safety. According to these officials, this is because civil federal aviation regulations require that aircraft control systems incorporate redundancies, meaning that failure of control cables would not cause loss of the airplane.[15]

The wire rope produced by Strandflex became the subject of a Defense Criminal Investigative Service investigation when the military discovered that it was not being tested to ensure that it met military specifications and an independent DOD test demonstrated that it did not meet strength requirements. The DOD Office of Inspector General (DODIG) notified the military services and FAA's Office of Civil Aviation Security at the same

---

[15]FAA officials also told us that civil aircraft cable assemblies are often designed to be five times stronger than they need to be. Furthermore, once aircraft control cables are assembled, they are tested in a manner that would reveal weaknesses in the wire rope.

time of potential problems with Strandflex.[16] The military services quickly addressed this situation by alerting responsible officials of the need to assess and address safety concerns associated with the use of this product. In contrast, as confirmed by a DOT Office of Inspector General's (DOTIG) investigation, FAA did not issue an Unapproved Parts Notification (UPN) to notify civil aviation community officials of potential problems with the Strandflex product for a year—a problem the inspector general attributed to weaknesses in the agency's overall processing of UPNs.[17] FAA officials acknowledged that there was a delay in issuing the UPN, but said that they had assessed the situation and concluded that it did not require urgent action.

Among other things, FAA did not inform the DOD Office of Inspector General (DODIG) that the appropriate recipient of its messages pertaining to suspect unapproved parts is its Suspect Unapproved Parts Program Office until the DOTIG initiated its investigation. While the DOTIG did not identify this as a key contributor to the year-long delay by FAA, even simple communication breakdowns such as not informing DOD of the appropriate addressee could lead to potential safety hazards being overlooked or going unreported to responsible officials.

Recognizing the fundamental nature of this shortcoming, the manager of FAA's Suspect Unapproved Parts Program Office cited a change in the FAA addressee as the first among numerous corrective actions that had been taken to address weaknesses identified by the DOTIG in the agency's processing of UPNs. Specifically, this manager advised the DOTIG general that the FAA copy of DOD alert messages would be sent directly to the Suspect Unapproved Parts Program Office rather than going through the Office of Civil Aviation Security. FAA and DOD officials told us that, while the Office of Civil Aviation Security remains the addressee on the official DOD notification letter to FAA, a facsimile copy is now sent directly to the Suspect Unapproved Parts Program Office. See appendix VIII for additional information on this case.

---

[16]DOD did not send its notification to FAA's program office primarily responsible for suspect unapproved parts. Rather it followed the standard procedure of transmitting it to FAA's Office of Civil Aviation Security and to the DOTIG.

[17]*OIG Investigation of Responses to Information About a Serious Flaw in Aircraft Cables*, U.S. Department of Transportation, Office of the Inspector General (Mar. 2, 2001, Report Number CC-2000-290).

Informal Channels of Communication Might Weaken As Key Personnel Retire

Some key individuals that have made informal communication on similar aviation safety issues effective between FAA and the military services have retired or can be expected to retire over the next several years. This makes succession planning an important part of aviation safety oversight for both departments.

Expected retirements among senior leaders over the next several years, along with recent and expected retirements among aviation safety personnel and senior leaders, may diminish the effectiveness of informal networks and make formal agency-based communication mechanisms even more important to the exchange of safety information between these entities. This is especially true, given that informal networks are sustained primarily by personal rather than agency-based relationships. The anticipated departure of these employees makes human capital planning an issue warranting management attention at both departments.

As we reported in April 2001,[18] DOD can expect 15 percent (over 45,000 employees) to retire by the end of fiscal year 2006. Retirements have already affected some senior aviation safety positions during the past year. For example, the key civilian at the Navy Safety Center retired in April 2001 and according to Naval safety officials a replacement was difficult to find due to the high demands of the job and lack of commensurate pay.[19] Similarly, one of the Army's key civilians in charge of aviation safety—responsible for the Safety of Flight Messages and routing FAA Airworthiness Directives to the appropriate aircraft program managers—has also retired. Army officials said that the departure of this individual has had little or no impact on the issuance of flight safety messages.[20] However, both of the retired aviation safety officials played a central role in the informal communication network for sharing aviation safety information among an extensive network of contacts both within and outside their respective services.

---

[18]*Federal Employee Retirements: Expected Increase Over the Next 5 Years Illustrates Need for Workforce Planning* (GAO-01-509, Apr. 27, 2001).

[19]A replacement began work in late August 2001.

[20]Among the military services, the Army has taken a unique step to develop and maintain the continuity of its aviation safety expertise by creating a separate career field for aviation safety at the Warrant Officer level. The other services typically rotate their military personnel through aviation safety positions or assign aviation safety as a collateral duty.

In recent years, we have increasingly stressed the need to plan for retirements within the federal government to help ensure the availability of adequately trained personnel. As we recently reported,[21] if federal employee retirements outpace the hiring of qualified replacement staff, the resulting loss of institutional knowledge and expertise could adversely affect mission achievement. This concern is especially great given that retirees often represent any agency's most experienced and knowledgeable staff. DOT is among the departments with a large number of personnel that will become eligible to retire over the next several years.

According to the *DOT 2000-2005 Strategic Plan*, the department plans to expand its workforce planning, including succession planning, for retirements in the next 10 years to ensure that DOT's staff has the skills and transportation competencies to accomplish its goals. Among these competencies, DOT has identified the Aviation Safety Series[22] job classification as a mission critical occupation important to succession planning. We estimate that 47 percent of the employees in this classification will be eligible to retire within the next 5 years.[23] In April 2001, we reported that almost 37 percent of DOT's workforce who are eligible to retire by the end of fiscal year 2006 would actually retire. Applying this percent of staff at DOT in the Aviation Safety Series who will be eligible to retire by the end of fiscal year 2006, we estimate that about 17 percent will actually retire. DOT will thus need to do succession planning for over 625 aviation safety positions.

Succession planning is one mechanism that FAA, DOD, and the military services can use to help ensure that effective informal networks are sustained and/or replenished in the wake of retirements of key aviation

---

[21]GAO-01-509, April 27, 2001.

[22]GS-1825—Aviation Safety Series includes positions that involve primarily developing, administering, or enforcing regulations and standards concerning civil aviation safety, including (1) the airworthiness of aircraft and aircraft systems; (2) the competence of pilots, mechanics, and other airmen; and (3) safety aspects of aviation facilities, equipment, and procedures. These positions require knowledge and skill in the operation, maintenance, or manufacture of aircraft and aircraft systems. As of September 30, 2000, FAA also had nine employees in the 1815 Air Safety Investigating Series, which are included in the percentages of safety employees eligible for retirement cited above.

[23]Retirement eligibility rates are calculated for those staff working as of September 30, 2000. Some of these staff might have retired between September 30, 2000, and September 10, 2001, when these numbers were calculated. Any other separations or new hires since 2000 are not reflected in these retirement rates.

safety personnel. However, succession planning can be difficult. To effectively deal with the expected retirements and other workforce challenges, an essential step for FAA and DOD is to engage in a planning process to identify human capital needs, assess how current staff and expected future staff will meet those needs, and create strategies to address any shortfalls or imbalances.

Necessary near-term steps for ensuring continuity of communication when key aviation safety personnel and senior leaders retire is (1) developing a common definition of aviation safety information of mutual concern, especially information deemed critical; (2) formalizing the channels of communication by creating an explicit process for exchanging all critical aviation safety information of mutual concern, including how specific aviation safety concerns were addressed; and (3) requiring that such information exchanges occur. Such action would also close gaps created by the current practice of sharing only some critical safety information on a formal, systematic, and timely basis.

FAA and DOD Recognize the Need to Formalize Communication, but Efforts to Date Have Not Addressed the Exchange of Critical Aviation Safety Information

FAA and DOD recognize the importance of formalizing communication on aviation issues to help ensure that communications outlast the tenure of specific individuals. This has been illustrated by efforts to develop more timely, systematic, and agency/service-based communication mechanisms through memorandums of agreement/understanding. For example, discussions are currently under way to determine what FAA's future role should be in certifying that military variants of civil aircraft meet the agency's aviation safety requirements.[24] However, these discussions between the departments to formalize communication channels do not include the broader issue of requiring a formal exchange of aviation safety information, in particular, that deemed critical.

Conclusions and Recommendations

Common aviation safety issues and responsibilities for safety oversight make the systematic and timely exchange of information a critical component of the aviation safety oversight systems of FAA and the military services. The informal and formal networks established by FAA

---

[24]The workload of FAA's certification staff is a central issue receiving attention. FAA currently provides airworthiness certification services to the military at no cost. Among the options currently being considered is an arrangement under which DOD would reimburse FAA for the services it provides. Otherwise, the military services would need to develop in-house expertise to certify civil aircraft types operated by the military.

GAO-02-77 Aviation Safety

and the military services to exchange critical aviation safety information have proven useful. However, because recent and expected retirements threaten to erode informal networks, additional formal channels of communication are needed to help ensure that safety risks common to both military and civil aircraft are identified and addressed in a formal, systematic, and timely manner. This includes the exchange of information on how FAA and the military services have addressed particular aviation safety concerns. Existing gaps in the formal processes used by FAA and the military services to exchange critical safety information—evidenced by the investigation of fuel tank flammability after the crash of TWA Flight 800 and the Strandflex case—could also allow for communication lapses and delays in getting critical safety information to the right parties in a timely manner, potentially resulting in the loss of lives and aircraft.

To help ensure the systematic exchange of critical safety information, we recommend that the Secretary of Defense and the Administrator of FAA, as directed by the Secretary of Transportation, develop a memorandum of agreement (MOA) that defines the types of safety information to be exchanged, the mechanisms for exchanging this information, and the parties responsible for this exchange. This MOA should also establish a mechanism for the two departments to exchange information on how they have responded to specific safety concerns.

Agency Comments

We provided a draft of this report to the secretary of DOD and the secretary of DOT for their review and comment. Both departments generally agreed with the report and provided written technical comments, which we have incorporated as appropriate. The Department of Defense agreed with our recommendation and the Department of Transportation agreed to consider it. See appendix IX for DOD's comments.

Copies of this report will be made available upon request. Please call me at (202) 512-2834 if you or your staff have any questions. Key contributors to this report are acknowledged in appendix X.

Peter F. Guerrrero
Director, Physical Infrastructure Issues

Appendix I: Objectives, Scope, and Methodology

For this assignment, we used a case study approach[25] supplemented by a review of the Federal Aviation Administration's (FAA) and Department of Defense's (DOD) aviation safety oversight processes and related interdepartmental communication efforts to (1) examine different responses by FAA and DOD/military services to similar aviation safety concerns and (2) assess the processes used by FAA and DOD to communicate about similar aviation safety concerns.[26] This report focuses primarily on safety issues pertaining to aircraft structures, parts, and materials that civil and military aviation have in common—not the safety of aircraft operations within the nation's air traffic control system. In addition, it does not address aviation security issues, such as hijacking, sabotage, or terrorist activities.

For the first objective, we chose case studies using two key selection criteria. First, we identified an aviation safety problem that was similar for both FAA and the military services. Second, we selected examples in which FAA and the DOD/military services had taken a different approach to solving a common aviation safety problem. After discussions with DOD and FAA, we selected case studies that pertain to aircraft wiring insulation and cockpit equipment designed to improve safety and support quality assurance programs for flight operations. The latter case study includes Ground Proximity Warning Systems, Traffic Alert and Collision Avoidance Systems, Flight Data Recorders, and Flight Operational Quality Assurance Programs. In conducting these case studies, we interviewed and requested documentation from officials with FAA, Air Force, Army, Marine Corps, Navy, Coast Guard, and others knowledgeable of their aviation safety oversight processes, including the National Transportation Safety Board, Flight Safety Foundation, National Aeronautics and Space Administration, Air Line Pilots Association, Air Transport Association, and aircraft manufacturers, and the DOT and DOD Offices of the Inspector General. In addition to our work in Washington, D.C., we also met with officials from each of the military services' safety centers and engineering organizations responsible for maintaining the safety of military aircraft, as well as officials from the William J. Hughes FAA Technical Center.

---

[25]The case studies selected represent a judgmental sample.

[26]For purposes of this report, we refer to FAA and the military services, rather than FAA and DOD. We recognize that DOD has ultimate authority for directing the services' actions on aviation safety oversight. Also, unless otherwise noted, the Coast Guard, which is a part of the Department of Transportation (DOT), is included under the discussions of the military services. Despite its peacetime missions, the Coast Guard's aviation safety oversight activities parallel those of the military services.

To answer the second objective, we interviewed the same officials cited under objective one. We also selected two other case studies that illustrate communication between FAA and the military services on aviation safety issues.

These include a discussion of a brand of control cable wire rope, which is used in the assembly of aircraft control cables, and the exchange of information between Air Force and civil aviation officials on fuel tank overheating in the E-4B, a military variant of the 747.

To determine the number and percent of DOT employees in the Aviation Safety job series who will be eligible to retire by the end of fiscal year 2006, we used data in the Office of Personnel Management's Central Personnel Data File (CPDF). Retirement eligibility dates were calculated using age at hire, years of service, birth date, and retirement plan coverage. Although we did not independently verify the DOT CPDF data, we had previously found that government-wide data from the CPDF for the key variables in this study (agency, birth date, service computation date, occupation, and retirement plan) were 99 percent or more accurate.[27]

We performed our work from November 2000 through January 2002 in accordance with generally accepted government auditing standards.

---

[27]*OPM's Central Personnel Data File: Data Appear Sufficiently Reliable to Meet Most Customer Needs* (GAO/GGD-98-199, Sept. 30, 1998).

Appendix II: Fixed Wing Military Aircraft and Their Civil Derivatives Operated by DOD

Military Aircraft Type/ Civilian Counterpart	Coast Guard	Army	Air Force	Navy/ Marines
E-3B/C AWACS (Boeing 707)			33	
E-4B (Boeing 747)			4	
VC-4A (Gulfstream I)	1			
E-6 A/B Mercury (Boeing 707)				16
E-8A/C JSTARS (Boeing 707)			4	
E-9A (de Havilland Dash 8, Model 102)			2	
C-9A/C (McDonnell Douglas DC-9)			23	
C-9B (McDonnell Douglas DC-9)				28
KC-10A (McDonnell Douglas DC-10-30-CF)			59	
C-12 (Beechcraft/Raytheon King Air)		122		
C-12C/D/F/J (Beechcraft/Raytheon King Air)			39	
RC-12 (Beechcraft/Raytheon King Air)		47		4
UC-12B/F/M Huron (Beechcraft/Raytheon King Air)				57
EC-18B (Boeing 707 ARIA)			3	
TC-18E (Boeing 707)			2	
UV-18B (de Havilland Twin Otter)			2	
C-20A/B (Gulfstream III)	1		8	
C-20 D/G (Gulfstream III, IV)		3		7
C-20H (Gulfstream IV)			2	
C-21A (Learjet 35A)			78	
C-22B (Boeing 727)			3	
C-23B+ Sherpa (Shorts)		43		
HU-25 Guardian (Falcon 20)	41			
VC-25 (Boeing 747-200B, Air Force One)			2	
C-26B/UC-26C Fairchild (Metro III)		11	12	7
VC-32A (Boeing 757-200)			4	
UC-35B/C Cessna Citation (560 Ultra)		23		8
C-37GV/A (Gulfstream V)	1		2	4
C-38A (Astra SPX -Israeli)			2	
C-40A Clipper (Boeing 737-700)				29
CT/T-43A (Boeing 737-200)			11	
C-130E/H (Lockheed Martin L-100)			525	
C-130T (Lockheed Martin L-100)				20
HC-130 Hercules (Lockheed Martin L-100)	30		34	
KC-130 F/R/T (Lockheed Martin L-100)				77
KC-130J (Lockheed Martin L-100)				52
C-150 (Cessna)			3	
T-1A (Beechjet 400T Jayhawk)			180	
T-3A Firefly (Slingsby T67M260)			114	
T-34C Turbomentor (Beechcraft Bonanza)				307
T-39 D/N/G (Rockwell Sabreliner)				26
T-41D (Cessna Mescalero C-172)			3	

Military Aircraft Type/ Civilian Counterpart	Coast Guard	Army	Air Force	Navy/ Marines
T-44A (King Air)				55
HH-65 Dolphin (Aerospatiale SA365N)	95			
HH-60J Jayhawk (Sikorsky S-70A)	42			
UH-60A Blackhawk (Sikorsky S-70A)		1,523		
HH/MH-60G Pavehawk (Sikorsky S-70A)			110	
CH-60S Knighthawk (Sikorsky S-70A)				247
HH-60H HCS (Sikorsky S-70B)				39
SH-60B/F Seahawk (Sikorsky S-70B)				232
SH-60R (Sikorsky S-70B)				248
TH-57 B/C Sea Ranger (Jet Ranger 206)				119
VH-60N Whitehawk (Sikorsky S-70A)				8
UH-1N/Y Iroquois (Bell Model 204/205)		Unknown	64	204

Appendix III: Key Similarities and Differences in FAA's and the Military Services' Aviation Safety Oversight Processes

The Federal Aviation Administration (FAA) and the military services share certain safety oversight systems, but three primary differences also exist. Similarities include common processes for disseminating safety information, managing aviation safety risks, and certifying that aircraft meet civil aviation safety standards. Differences include processes to certify that aircraft meet their unique safety standards and to investigate aircraft accidents, as well as timetables and thresholds for making decisions about potential aviation safety problems.

Internal Mechanisms to Communicate Safety-Related Information Are Similar

FAA and the military services have both created formal and informal internal mechanisms to implement their aviation safety oversight programs.

Formal internal mechanisms are used to communicate official information, such as orders and directives. For example, FAA issues Airworthiness Directives (ADs) to provide primarily owners and operators of civil aircraft with formal notice of an unsafe condition. For large civil commercial aircraft,[28] ADs are written by the agency's Transport Airplane Directorate Aircraft Certification Service in Renton, Washington, and sent to FAA's Oklahoma City office, which has responsibility for formal distribution to owners and operators of registered civil aircraft and the posting of this information to the FAA Web site. Similarly, the military services issue near-equivalents of ADs to distribute aviation safety messages to affected units and sister services' aviation safety centers. In addition, the chiefs of the military services' safety centers hold a Joint Services Safety Conference every six months.

According to both FAA and military officials, formal communication mechanisms also include internal meetings among engineering and program staff as well as FAA senior managers or internal meetings of senior military officers responsible for aviation safety. Both use training as another means of formally sharing aviation safety information internally among agency/service staff.

---

[28]The Transport Airplane Directorate issues ADs for airplanes type certificated under 14 C.F.R. 25, which includes large commercial aircraft and many smaller business jets. The Small Airplane Directorate in Kansas City, Missouri, issues ADs for airplanes type certificated under a separate regulation (14 C.F.R. 23), which include many airplanes in commercial service some of which are considered commuter airplanes. Other directorates issue ADs for rotorcraft, engines, and propellers. The directorate of the geographical area in which the manufacturer is located normally issues ADs for appliances and parts.

Both FAA and the military services also have internal informal networks in place among aviation safety personnel that are used to share information. These exchanges are typically self-initiated, occur on an ad hoc basis, and are based largely on personal relationships. It is a primary means used among the military services' safety centers to keep apprised of current aviation safety issues. According to FAA and military aviation safety officials, personal relationships are a cornerstone of informal communication within both FAA and the military services and have resulted in extensive networking that allows for an active exchange of aviation safety information.

FAA and the Military Services Use a Similar Process for Managing Aviation Safety Risks

FAA and the military services all use variations of a five-step process for managing aviation safety risks.[29]

(1) *Identifying potential aviation safety risks*. FAA and the military services employ similar proactive and reactive methods for identifying potential aviation safety risks. For example, they monitor pilots' reports of aircraft performance problems, manufacturers' recommendations, foreign civil and military aviation authorities' reports, mechanics' reports of aircraft structural, part, or material weaknesses, inspectors' reports of aircraft conditions and maintenance records, and information exchanges between stakeholders (e.g., airlines, pilots, and engineers) in the aviation community. Reactive methods include actions taken as the result of findings and recommendations from aircraft mishaps and accident investigations.

(2) *Assessing safety risks to determine if corrective action is warranted*. Both FAA and the military services assess the safety risks of a potential aviation safety problem to determine if action is warranted. This includes weighing the costs and benefits that taking action might have in mitigating or eliminating a safety risk and fulfilling their

---

[29]Technically, the Army (1) identifies hazards, (2) assesses hazards, (3) develops controls and makes decisions, (4) implements controls, and (5) supervises and evaluates. The Air Force has further divided these steps to create a six-step process: (1) identify hazards, (2) assess risks, (3) analyze risk control measures, (4) make control decisions, (5) implement risk control, and (6) supervise and review [implementation of control measures]. The Coast Guard uses a seven-step process: (1) identify mission tasks, (2) identify hazards, (3) assess risks, (4) identify options, (5) evaluate risk versus gain, (6) execute decision, and (7) monitor situation. FAA's process includes (1) receiving and compiling problem reports; (2) evaluating the impact on safety, which includes an assessment of associated risk; (3) determining what, if any, corrective action is warranted; and (4) implementing corrective action (e.g., issuing an AD).

responsibilities. For example, this process assists military decision-makers in choosing if and how much to fund a project and in comparing its urgency to other projects competing for resources.

DOD requires the military services to use risk management and accident investigations as decision-making tools for identifying potential safety problems, assessing safety risks, and implementing and monitoring corrective actions.[30] FAA requires the use of safety risk management by all offices, consistent with their role within the agency.[31]

FAA and the military services commonly use a risk assessment matrix to estimate the level of risk associated with a potential or identified aviation safety risk. The safety risk is estimated in terms of its probability and severity. For example, FAA and the Air Force use a risk matrix to classify identified or potential safety problems into one of four categories of risk— extremely high, high, medium, and low. FAA and military service officials acknowledge that some of the components used to prepare this type of safety risk estimate are subjective but, to the extent practical, they rely on technical experts to inform the decision-making process.

An assessment of safety risk may lead decision-makers to conclude that no action is warranted or that the implementation of measures to mitigate a problem will achieve an acceptable level of safety risk. For example, according to Air Force safety officials, if a major command concludes that a risk to life, health, property or environment posed by the operation of an aircraft system or subsystem falls within acceptable limits—without mitigation or upon completion of mitigation efforts—a formal decision will likely be made to accept the residual risk.

Assessments of risks associated with aircraft safety can vary among FAA and the military services, even when they share a similar safety hazard. According to FAA and military officials, this variability can be attributed, in part, to differences in missions, operating environments, and aircraft operational practices.

---

[30]Department of Defense Instruction, DOD Safety and Occupational Health Program, Number 6055.1, August 19, 1998 and Department of Defense Instruction, Accident Investigation, Reporting, and Record Keeping, Number 6055.7, October 3, 2000.

[31]FAA Order 8040.4 requires that safety risk management be used for all high consequence decisions ($100 million per year) and requires a formal, documented plan/process for each staff office and line of business.

(3) ***Determining a corrective course of action to be taken***. According to FAA and military officials, when determining the appropriate course of action to address a potential or identified aviation safety hazard, their organizations consult with technical experts, including engineers, manufacturers' representatives, pilots, and maintenance personnel. These experts identify a range of potential remedies, weigh the costs and benefits of each remedy, and select the most appropriate course of action to minimize danger to air crews and damage to aircraft by eliminating a safety risk or achieving an acceptable level of residual risk. For example, following the crash of Alaska Air Flight 261 on January 31, 2000, FAA determined that an emergency AD was warranted to inspect several McDonnell Douglas aircraft for excessive wear of their jackscrew assemblies on the horizontal stabilizer. Such wear could severely limit the ability of aircrews to control an airplane and posed an unacceptable level of risk to flight safety.

The military services follow a similar process. For example, according to a senior Army safety official, once Army engineers from the Aviation and Missile Command (AMCOM) have determined an appropriate course of action for a given aviation safety hazard, they prepare a narrative describing to field personnel the precise remedy that they are ordered to implement. This narrative also indicates whether the action is an interim or final approach for reducing the hazard. AMCOM engineers may require the replacement of a defective part immediately; the operation of aircraft at or below a prescribed speed; more frequent inspections of aircraft; or that the aircraft be grounded immediately. The Army took the last action in June 2001, when investigators in Israel discovered damage to an Apache helicopter's tail rotor after a low number of flight hours. In response, AMCOM engineers decided that the potential risk to flight safety warranted grounding the majority of the Army's fleet of Apache helicopters to allow tail rotors that had been in service for greater than 1000 hours to be x-rayed immediately.

(4) ***Implementing corrective actions***. According to FAA and military officials, their organizations also have similar methods to implement corrective actions to address a potential or identified aviation safety problem. Corrective actions can be taken to restore the safety of approved products to the level of safety required by airworthiness standards (e.g., through the issuance of an AD by FAA) or to upgrade airworthiness standards through the issuance of new rules that will apply to aircraft at

some future date. For example, FAA issues an AD to notify primarily civil aircraft owners and operators of an unsafe condition and to mandate a specific corrective action.[32] The military services issue their respective equivalents. Both identify required actions and time frames for implementing those actions.

Depending on the perceived level of safety risk to flight operations, a directive may require corrective action once a certain number of flight hours has been reached. Physical inspections might determine if a problem exists on a given aircraft, if a certain part must be repaired or replaced, or if the installation of equipment is required. Alternatively, a directive may place restrictions on certain flight maneuvers, while continuing to permit an unlimited number of flight operations. Finally, a directive may not be deemed necessary and an advisory message issued instead. Such advisories are designed to alert flight crews and maintenance personnel to potential equipment defects or limitations.

When FAA determines that action is warranted, it may develop a regulation through the federal rulemaking process. As we recently reported,[33] in doing so, it must balance the potential consequences for the aviation community and the nation with the consequences of inaction on public safety. On the one hand, the process of developing regulations, or rulemaking, is complex and time-consuming. Because rules can have a significant impact on individuals, industries, the economy, and the environment, proposed rules must be carefully considered before being finalized. On the other hand, threats to public safety and the rapid pace of technological development in the aviation industry demand timely action. A need for rulemaking can be identified internally, by one of FAA's offices, or externally, by an outside source such as Congress through a statutory mandate or the National Transportation Safety Board (NTSB) through a recommended rulemaking. When the Congress mandates a rulemaking, FAA is required to initiate the process. When NTSB issues a recommendation, FAA studies the situation and decides whether to initiate the rulemaking process.

---

[32]The FAA Aircraft Certification Service also issues Special Airworthiness Information Bulletins to communicate information to enhance safety, but not to mandate that a specific action be taken.

[33]*Aviation Rulemaking: Further Reform Is Needed to Address Long-standing Problems* (GAO-01-821, July 9, 2001).

Both FAA and the military services maintain emergency procedures to compel immediate action. If FAA determines, for example, that a serious threat of an unsafe condition exists, the agency may decide to issue an emergency AD. This process allows FAA to issue an emergency directive first and submit it for stakeholders' comments and potential revision at a later date. Issuance of an emergency AD can require that aircraft operators comply before making their next flight.

Each branch of the military maintains a similar emergency process. For example, the Army may issue an Emergency Safety of Flight Message that immediately grounds all affected aircraft. The Air Force and Coast Guard, likewise, signal an emergency situation by publishing a Time Compliance Technical Order. The Navy issues a message called a Bulletin Technical Directive (Immediate Compliance).

(5) *Monitoring to ensure that corrective actions have been taken*. Both FAA and the military services monitor compliance with required corrective actions largely through inspections and audits. For example, federal law establishes that the airlines are responsible for providing service with the highest possible degree of safety in the public interest and FAA is responsible for, among other things, overseeing airlines' compliance with the statute and regulations. This includes, for example, examining airlines' operations when they seek a certificate to operate and for conducting periodic inspections to oversee airlines' continued compliance with safety regulations. FAA also tracks various reports from flight crews to monitor airline compliance with FAA requirements.

Similarly, the military services also rely upon inspections and audits to ensure that corrective actions have been implemented. Compliance measures include recording in aircraft logbooks or other official documents that corrective actions have been taken and, in some cases, reporting compliance directly to the responsible oversight organization by unique aircraft identification numbers.

The Military Services Adhere to FAA's Regulations to Establish and Maintain the Airworthiness of Some Military Aircraft That Are Civil Variants

The military services use FAA's civil aircraft certification services to establish the airworthiness of some similar aircraft types (e.g., the civil variant of the Air Force's T-43 is the Boeing 737 commercial aircraft) and can retain this certification by maintaining the aircraft in accordance with the civil federal aviation regulations. FAA has responsibility for certifying that civil aircraft meet federal airworthiness requirements. To document that aircraft comply with these requirements, the agency issues type (aircraft design), production, and airworthiness certificates for aircraft produced by civil aircraft manufacturers in the United States. In some cases, FAA may issue aircraft type, production, and airworthiness certificates for a military variant of a civil aircraft as well as supplemental type certificates when modifications to an aircraft are made, but still meet civil airworthiness standards.[34] See figure 1. Discussions among senior FAA and DOD officials are under way to determine FAA's future role in certifying that military aircraft that are variants of civil aircraft comply with FAA's minimum safety requirements. Some consideration is being given to the military reimbursing FAA for its certification services.

---

[34]The Coast Guard does not certify the airworthiness of aircraft in a similar manner to FAA. While FAA certification is sometimes a requirement for the aircraft it purchases, subsequent changes to aircraft do not receive such certification.

Figure 1: Examples of FAA Involvement in Certifying Air Force Aircraft as Airworthy

KC-10, C-32, C-20, C-37

Joint-Stars, Airborne Laser Aircraft

F-117, F-15, F-16, B-1, B-2, many others

- FAA certified Type Design (basic airplane) maintained throughout service life

- Provided airworthiness, test engineering, and production staff to certify aircraft design

- Air Force responsible for mission suitability and effect

- Basic airplane FAA certified

- Modifications more extensive than FAA is willing to certify

- Air Force responsible for mission airworthiness and quality of all modifications

- No FAA certification involved

- Air Force operators/acquirers determine and contract for requirement

Heavy FAA Involvement ⟶ **No FAA Involvement**

Source: U.S. Air Force.

| Different Methods Are Used to Certify the Airworthiness of Military Aircraft That Do Not Meet Civil Standards | Different certification methods are used when military aircraft derived from civil variants are modified for mission-readiness purposes to the extent that they no longer meet civil standards for airworthiness and when an aircraft is operated exclusively by the military (e.g., fighter aircraft).[35] In such cases, DOD engineers must use their own standards to certify that an aircraft meets requirements for the minimum level of safety. For example, if the military modifies a C-130 (a variant of the civil L-100) to convert it |

---

[35]There is no requirement that the military services maintain their civil derivative aircraft in accordance with FAA standards. However, doing so allows an aircraft to be sold for use in civil aviation at a later date.

from a passenger-carrying aircraft to one used for air-to-air aircraft refueling, the modifications would not meet civil airworthiness standards. Consequently, DOD engineers would assume responsibility for certifying the airworthiness of this aircraft and it would no longer maintain its safety certification for civil use. In contrast to FAA's aircraft certification procedures, the military services serve as both the approving officials and the ultimate users of military aircraft. In addition, the approval process must consider not only the safety and airworthiness of an aircraft, but also its suitability and effectiveness to meet mission readiness requirements. Furthermore, the military services do not issue certificates documenting that military aircraft meet military standards for aircraft type (design), aircraft production, and airworthiness.

Civil and Military Accident Investigation Processes Differ

A second key difference is the accident investigation process: the military services conduct their own accident investigations while civil aviation accident investigations are conducted primarily by an independent agency, NTSB.[36] Following an aircraft accident, the military conducts a "safety investigation" to determine the cause of an accident, followed by a separate "legal accident investigation" to obtain and preserve evidence for the chain of command and for use in litigation, claims, disciplinary action or adverse administrative actions against flight crews.[37] In contrast, the NTSB, which has the authority to conduct all civil accident investigations, performs a single investigation following an aircraft accident. FAA conducts the on-site investigations in most (80 percent) of general aviation accidents and submits a factual report to NTSB. During accident investigations, FAA looks into the potential roles of the air traffic control system, navigational aids, pilots' flight and medical qualifications, as well as the adequacy of the agency's rules and whether or not those rules were followed.

The reports of military "safety investigations" contain two types of information—nonprivileged and privileged. Nonprivileged data, such as

---

[36]Under 49 USC 1131 (a)(2)(B), the NTSB will surrender lead investigation status on a transportation accident when the attorney general, in consultation with the chairman of the Safety Board, notifies the board that circumstances reasonably indicate that the accident may have been caused by an intentional criminal act. At this point, the Federal Bureau of Investigation takes over the investigation, and the NTSB only provides requested support.

[37]Following aircraft accidents, the military services' "safety investigations" are conducted strictly for mishap prevention purposes, while "legal investigations" (also known as collateral investigations) cover all other issues related to an accident.

engineering analyses, may be released to the public. Privileged data,[38] such as confidential witness statements[39] made by flight crew members, reluctant witnesses, and some contractors, are not made accessible to the public or used in litigation, claims, disciplinary actions or other adverse administrative actions.[40] The intent of this discretion is to quickly identify root causes by encouraging candor among flight crews and witnesses to prevent similar accidents in the future and to help ensure military readiness. In contrast, during the civil version of the "safety investigation" by the NTSB, the only protection against potential criminal action available to civil commercial pilots is refusing to be interviewed or testify.

Pace of Decisionmaking and Thresholds for Safety Actions Differ for Military and Civil Aviation

The pace with which FAA and the military services make decisions about potential and identified aviation safety concerns differs, as do the thresholds used to determine that action is warranted. For example, the command and control structure of the military services allows immediate action, such as the grounding of a fleet of aircraft, after considering the impact on their respective missions, but without consulting outside entities or considering economic impact. In contrast, while FAA can and has taken similar immediate action, the agency must also weigh the potential ramifications for the nation's economy. Arriving at such a decision may involve consultation with manufacturers, operators, and other aviation stakeholders. Such consultation and coordination can take place at a very rapid pace when dictated by an unsafe condition.

FAA and DOD operate under different formal requirements for issuing aviation safety regulations. For example, when DOD issues an order to address an aviation safety hazard, the military services are required to issue instructions implementing the order, which are effective upon signature by the approving official. In contrast, FAA, as a regulator of civil aircraft, must often follow a complex rulemaking process (except in emergency situations). This includes providing a full and open notice and

---

[38]While there is no equivalent "privilege" protection for civil aviation, there are some provisions for protecting the disclosure of data, such as closing some parts of the court docket and disallowing the release of cockpit voice recordings.

[39]Witness statements taken during "safety investigations" are deemed privileged only if a promise of confidentiality is made.

[40]Privileged material also includes deliberative and pre-decisional information that is safeguarded to ensure a candid exchange among parties in the "safety investigation" report prior to final approval.

comment period for stakeholders to help ensure that all aspects of any
regulatory change are fully analyzed before the change goes into effect. As
we recently reported, from fiscal year 1995 through fiscal year 2000, FAA
took about 2-1/2 years on average to proceed from formal initiation of the
rulemaking process through publication of the final rule—a process it
completed for 29 significant rules. However, for 6 of these rules it took 10
years or more to complete this process.[41] Furthermore, the thresholds used
by FAA and the military services to determine when and if a potential or
identified aviation safety problem should be addressed also vary due
primarily to mission differences. FAA's primary mission is safety, while the
military services must weigh multiple mission-readiness requirements
against taking action to maximize aviation safety.

[41]*Aviation Rulemaking: Further Reform Is Needed to Address Long-standing Problems*
(GAO-01-821, July 9, 2001).

Appendix IV: Case Study on Aromatic Polyimide Wire Insulation

In the mid-1980s, the Navy began experiencing problems with aromatic polyimide, a general purpose wire insulator (commonly known as Kapton[42]), that it did not fully understand. In response, the Navy enlisted the assistance of experts from other military services and the Federal Aviation Administration (FAA) to better characterize the problems and develop possible solutions. Ultimately, FAA and each of the military services responded differently to the problems of aromatic polyimide.

Aromatic polyimide is the most commonly used wire insulation on many older Boeing and McDonnell Douglas airplanes that were built beginning in the late 1960s.[43] It is lightweight, resistant to abrasion and cuts, is able to withstand high temperatures, and is flame and environmentally resistant. However, two weaknesses have also been documented. First, water alters the chemical composition of this insulation and diminishes its integrity. A second weakness occurs when two cracks in the insulation occur close together, enabling the current to arc between the cracks (arcing events) at high temperatures.[44] Exposure to this heat causes the insulation to "carbonize" and actually become a conductor rather than an insulator.

United States Navy

The Navy started using aromatic polyimide in the mid-1970s, began noticing cracks and breaks in the top coats of this insulation in 1980 and 1981, and undertook research to identify potential problems with its use. In 1984, researchers at the Naval Research Laboratory reported that moisture caused aromatic polyimide to break down when it was exposed to high humidity, moisture, or water for long periods of time. It also found that carbon deposits can form and build up between two cracks in this insulation after several arcing events, a process that ultimately trips a circuit breaker. When a pilot presses a tripped circuit breaker to reset it, an entire wire bundle can be disabled, potentially causing catastrophic results.

---

[42]Kapton is Dupont's trade name for a specific type of wire insulation, known as aromatic polyimide, which is also made by another manufacturer. Aromatic polyimide will be referred to throughout this report in place of Kapton, its military specification (MIL-W-81381) or Boeing's Military Specification (BMS 13-51).

[43]The wire was initially produced in 1966 and used in Lockheed L-1011s, Douglas MD-80s and MD-11s, Boeing 727s, 737s, 747s, 757s, 767s, Grumman F-14s, McDonnell F-15s and F/A-18s, and General Dynamics F-16s.

[44]Arc-tracking temperatures vary according to wire size and the amount of electrical current.

In December 1985, the Navy decided that aromatic polyimide would no longer be its wiring insulator of choice. Subsequently, the Navy selectively removed this wire insulation from parts of aircraft where it was most problematic, such as fore and aft flaps, wheel wells, and around unsecured seals that could leak. However, because the Navy still had a large supply of aromatic polyimide on hand, it continued its use on aircraft in areas that were not vulnerable to water infiltration. The Navy also took delivery of some McDonnell Douglas aircraft in 1988 that were built with aromatic polyimide wiring insulation that had been purchased before problems with this wire insulation were recognized.

United States Coast Guard

In 1993, the Coast Guard also developed problems with aromatic polyimide on its fleet of H-65 Dolphin helicopters. These helicopters are exposed to a significant amount of water during normal operations, such as from swimmers undergoing rescue training and individuals rescued. In addition, many of these helicopters often spend as long as 6 months patrolling at sea where they are constantly exposed to salt spray and salt water.

Between 1993 and 1996, some serious events of in-flight fires resulting in cockpit smoke and fumes occurred in the Coast Guard's H-65 helicopters. Some of these mishaps led to loss of all electrically powered flight instruments. One incident (at low altitude, over water, in fog, and at dusk) nearly resulted in the loss of helicopter and crew. While no helicopters were destroyed as a result of cockpit fires, the Coast Guard decided to take precautionary measures to reduce the likelihood of future fires in these helicopters by systematically removing aromatic polyimide. In 1994, they began replacing this type of wire insulation during the H-65's regularly scheduled forty-eight month maintenance cycle and according to a senior Coast Guard safety official, completed this removal in September 2001.

United States Air Force

According to an Air Force wiring expert, the Air Force also experienced failures associated with aromatic polyimide and took steps to mitigate them. It was also aware of the concerns raised by the Navy and sponsored a research program that led to the development of a composite wiring construction (Teflon-Kapton-Teflon) that mitigated many of the problems exhibited by aromatic polyimide. In October 1988, the Air Force chief of staff issued a policy statement on aromatic polyimide that no perfect wire exists and such requirements as operational performance, maintenance, logistics needs, resistance to combat damage, and safety and environmental aspects must be considered when choosing a wire. Aromatic polyimide would no longer be considered the wire of first choice for new systems, modifications, or rewiring applications, and not be used in severe wind and moisture-prone (SWAMP) areas or in locations with frequent flexing. However, wholesale removal of aromatic polyimide was not planned. This policy remains in force.

United States Army

In response to potential hazards identified by the Navy with the use of aromatic polyimide, the Army conducted further testing in 1986 and confirmed the Navy's findings. In 1988, the Army concluded that it did not have the same problems with aromatic polyimide that the Navy did and determined that no action was necessary. The Army attributed the Navy's problems with this insulation to its operating environment, in particular the long-term exposure of its aircraft to salt water.

The Army's Aviation Missile Command (AMCOM) officials decided that the use of aromatic polyimide in Army helicopters was not a primary safety issue. While the Army had experienced some wiring-related problems, there was no evidence linking them to aromatic polyimide. The Army did have durability concerns; however, it found the degree to which aromatic polyimide chafes in Apache and Blackhawk helicopters is unacceptable over the long-term. The Army did not order the immediate removal of this wire insulation, but has decided to strip it from aircraft when they are refurbished. As of June 2001, aromatic polyimide had been removed from 1,389 of the 1,523 Blackhawk helicopters in the Army's fleet. According to an AMCOM official, current funding is sufficient to remove this wire insulation from only 4 of the 134 remaining Blackhawks.

AMCOM also conducted a system safety risk assessment on aromatic polyimide for its Blackhawk helicopters, issued in July 2001. The assessment concluded the most appropriate action is to replace Kapton (aromatic polyimide) wiring with non-Kapton wiring during scheduled upgrades or any time the aircraft is sent into a depot to be rebuilt, overhauled, or refurbished. This approach would allow all aircraft that are currently wired with Kapton to be upgraded to non-Kapton wiring by 2008.

Federal Aviation Administration

FAA wiring experts reported that they were aware of only one incident on a commercial aircraft linked to aromatic polyimide wire insulation. In 1985, a Boeing 757, operated by Monarch Airlines in the United Kingdom, experienced an arc-tracking event in aromatic polyimide wire insulation after circuits were tripped, and smoke appeared in flight. Investigators

suspect that the wire bundle was damaged when it was marked with a hot
stamping tool and subsequently came into contact with fluid leaking from
a lavatory.

FAA has not mandated the removal of aromatic polyimide from
commercial aircraft. The agency, however, has issued three advisory
circulars (AC) on wiring practices: (1) in March 1987, FAA issued AC 25-10
to provide guidance on the installation of miscellaneous, nonrequired
electrical equipment; (2) in April 1991, the agency issued AC 25-16 on
electrical fault and fire prevention and protection, including the need to
keep aromatic polyimide away from moisture-prone areas; and (3) in
September 1998, FAA issued AC 43.13-1B to describe acceptable methods,
techniques, and practices for aircraft inspection and repair, including
wires insulated with aromatic polyimide.

In addition, FAA's Technical Center conducted studies on arc tracking
under wet conditions in August 1988 and found, among other things, that
certain polyimide (including aromatic polyimide) wire insulation
constructions can be modified to resist wet-wire arc tracking by applying
thin protective coatings. It conducted an additional study on arcing events
under dry conditions in July 1989 and found that severe dry arc tracking
occurred for all aromatic polyimide samples, with extensive damage to all
wires in the bundles. This was followed by a study of electrical short
circuit[45] and current overload tests on aircraft wiring in March 1995. This
study found that circuit breakers provide reliable protection against
excessive or dangerous rises in temperature in the conductor or its
insulation caused by direct short circuits.

A senior FAA official stressed that improved safety margins can be
achieved by measures other than wire replacement: use of enhanced
circuit protection, increased separation of wires, removal of flammable
materials, or protection of wires from moisture. These methods may be
more effective than wholesale modification or re-manufacture.

The same official told us that the rules that admitted aromatic polyimide
20 years ago would prohibit it today because of the failure modes that
have been identified. Much more is known now about the limitations of
this type of wire insulation, specifically that it has the potential to arc

---

[45]A short circuit occurs when there is an abnormal connection between two points of a
circuit that results in excess and often damaging flow of current between these points.

track and can contribute to a single event or combination of events that could be a hazard to aircraft. According to this official, given current knowledge, it would be difficult for FAA to support the use of aromatic polyimide insulation, in its original form, in new aircraft designs. However, this same official noted that while new wire insulation types introduced on the market are likely to have improved performance characteristics, they are also likely to have shortcomings not anticipated at their introduction into service.

Boeing Commercial Group

In response to the Navy's problems with aromatic polyimide, Boeing conducted laboratory experiments in 1985 and 1986 and found that they could simulate arc tracking in Boeing commercial aircraft. Boeing officials told us that they immediately notified Dupont Chemical Corporation, the manufacturer of Kapton (aromatic polyimide). Boeing officials also told us that the company wanted to anticipate any potential FAA rulemaking on aromatic polyimide and began using a new wire insulator known as BMS-60, or Teflon-Kapton-Teflon (TKT), in 1993. This wire retained aromatic polyimide's favorable mechanical qualities while embedding the aromatic polyimide between layers of Teflon to strengthen it. Boeing still uses aromatic polyimide for wiring to power feeders that run from a set of engines into a power panel. These runs are long and do not require that the wire be bent; Boeing reported that it has not found any instances of cracks or arc tracking in these areas.

Joint Military/FAA/Industry Efforts

In February 1997, the White House Commission on Aviation Safety and Security issued a report to President Clinton identifying aging wiring as a safety issue in aviation. The Commission recommended that three federal agencies—FAA, Department of Defense, and National Aeronautics and Space Administration—expand their aging aircraft program to include the issue of aging wire systems in commercial aircraft. These agencies have established research initiatives and partnerships with industry to address wiring issues in aging aircraft as a part of ongoing informal coordination and in response to this recommendation.

In October of 1998, the director of Navy Safety and System Survivability established a government and industry forum, known as the Aircraft Wiring and Inert Gas Generator Working Group (AWIGG), to (1) ensure that information on aircraft wiring and fire suppression is shared and understood by all interested parties and (2) combine the resources of interested participants to accelerate the development of aviation safety technologies. AWIGG membership now totals more than 350 individuals, representing military services, airlines, aircraft and wire manufacturers, pilots and mechanics unions, researchers, FAA, National Transportation Safety Board, NASA, and others.

In October 1998, FAA established the Aging Transport System Rulemaking Advisory Committee (ATSRAC)[46] to serve the public interest by providing a forum for interaction among FAA, the military, NASA, the airlines, airline pilots, manufacturers, and their representatives on aging aircraft. FAA believed that the level of expertise and balanced viewpoint of this committee would enable early identification of potential problem areas and accelerate development of cost-effective corrective actions. Under ATSRAC two separate working groups were created—one to conduct visual (nonintrusive) inspections and another to conduct comprehensive physical (intrusive) inspections of aging aircraft wiring.

One ATSRAC working group conducted visual (nonintrusive) inspections of eighty-one in-service aircraft that were over twenty years old. The working group was comprised of lead airline representatives from each of the fleet types, the airframe manufacturers, and FAA. The purpose of these inspections was to assess the condition of the U.S. transport fleet with respect to wiring, identify areas of concern, and make recommendations, if necessary. The results were released August 1, 2000, and found that the majority of discrepancies with wire were in areas of frequent maintenance activity where wiring was unprotected from debris and fluid contamination.

To complement and extend the results of the nonintrusive inspections, ATSRAC requested a joint working group effort to conduct extensive physical (intrusive) inspections of aging aircraft wiring systems. FAA conducted this work in conjunction with ATA and with the support of the Navy and Air Force. Intrusive inspections were performed on six recently decommissioned airplanes to assess the conditions of the electrical wiring on aged airplanes.[47, 48] The results were released December 29, 2000. The working group report identified two items that FAA should pursue

---

[46]In June 1998, the Air Transport Association (ATA) formed the Aging Systems Task Force. The group was later cosponsored and rechartered by the Aging Transport Systems Rulemaking Advisory Committee.

[47]The six airplane models used were two DC-9s, one DC-10, one 747, one L-1011, and one A300.

[48]This second major inspection effort was entitled the Intrusive Inspection Working Group.

aggressively to develop options to eliminate or mitigate electrical hazards: arc-fault circuit breakers and nondestructive test equipment for aircraft wiring. An arc-fault circuit breaker is being developed by a number of government and industry organizations, including the Navy and FAA. This type of circuit breaker can detect and react to an electrical arc much faster than those currently used in aircraft today. When an arc is detected, this type of circuit breaker can disable the circuit and provide a warning that a fault exists. The report did not recommend systematic removal of aromatic polyimide from aging aircraft.

The report also included a dissenting opinion from one of the working group members. Among other things, this member contended that (1) the data collection and analysis was seriously flawed, that the group inappropriately reinterpreted data and that they had little or no opportunity to review and validate the original data; (2) there was a lack of rigor in the process as demonstrated by informal, changing, or imprecise definition of terms; (3) the testing protocols were not executed rigorously; and (4) certain findings were not classified appropriately. The working group disagreed with these and other criticisms raised by this member, responded formally to them in the report, and invited other interested parties to read both the report and the dissenting opinion to ascertain the merits of each.

Appendix V: Case Study on Adoption of Cockpit Safety Equipment

Beginning in the early 1970s, a number of studies looked into the occurrence of accidents where a properly functioning aircraft under the control of a fully qualified and certified crew flew into terrain with no awareness by the crew. According to the Flight Safety Foundation, this type of accident represents the single largest safety risk to aircraft. In the mid-1980s, the high number of aircraft accidents caused by midair collisions also became a central concern for aviation safety. To address these safety issues, the Federal Aviation Administration (FAA) required the installation of Ground Proximity Warning Systems (GPWS) on most passenger-carrying aircraft to alert pilots to potential collisions with terrain and Traffic Alert and Collision Avoidance Systems (TCAS) to warn pilots of potential airborne collisions with other aircraft and provide them with information to take evasive action.[49] The military services have moved more slowly to install similar safety equipment in their passenger-and troop-carrying aircraft due to resource tradeoffs between aviation safety and other mission-readiness issues.

FAA Has Required GPWS Aboard Passenger-Carrying Aircraft Since the 1970s

In 1974, as a result of studies and recommendations from the National Transportation Safety Board, FAA required all operators of large turbine-powered airplanes and some operators of large turbojet airplanes to install approved GPWS equipment. In 1978, the FAA extended the GPWS requirement to operators of smaller airplanes and turbojet-powered airplanes with ten or more passenger seats. In 1992, in response to studies by the NTSB, FAA required GPWS equipment on all turbine-powered airplanes with 10 or more passenger seats.

Advances in terrain mapping technology led to the development of a new type of ground proximity warning system that provides greater awareness for flight crews. FAA ultimately approved the advanced equipment known as the enhanced ground proximity warning system (EGPWS).[50] EGPWS equipment standards have been improved to provide flight crews with earlier auditory and visual warnings of terrain, forward-looking capability,

---

[49]Specifically, TCAS I provides pilots with nonverbal alerts of potential collisions, while the more advanced version, TCAS II, provides pilots with verbal advice to execute an evasive maneuver (e.g., "climb," "descend," or "do nothing") to avoid other aircraft.

[50]Because FAA expected that a variety of EGPWS technologies could be developed that would meet the improved standards, it is currently using the broader term "terrain awareness and warning system (TAWS)."

and additional time to take corrective actions in a more smooth and gradual manner.

In 1996, a FAA study concluded that existing GPWS would have prevented 75 percent of 44 accidents that occurred on smaller capacity aircraft between 1985 and 1994, while EGPWS would have prevented 95 percent of those accidents. A second study, focusing on the merits of retrofitting large-capacity scheduled and unscheduled airline fleets with EGPWS, showed that four of nine accidents, or 44 percent, should have been prevented by the basic GPWS if it had been functioning or utilized properly. The study concluded that the EGPWS technology would have prevented all nine of those accidents.

In 1998, FAA issued a draft rule proposing that all turbine-powered U.S. airplanes registered with FAA that have six or more passenger seats be equipped with a FAA approved EGPWS. On March 29, 2000, the agency issued the final rule mandating the installation of EGPWS equipment on all such aircraft.[51] The new regulation applies immediately to those aircraft built after March 29, 2002. Aircraft manufactured on or before March 29, 2002, will be required to comply by March 29, 2005.

FAA Has Required TCAS Installation Since the Late 1980s

For the past 13 years, FAA has taken active steps to require installation of TCAS on commercial passenger aircraft. Following a 1986 midair collision between two commercial aircraft in California, Congress passed a law in 1987 requiring FAA to mandate the use of TCAS. In January 1989, the agency published a rule requiring installation and use of TCAS II (enhanced version) in commercial passenger-carrying aircraft and TCAS I in commuter aircraft with 10 to 30 passenger seats. By 1993, all air carrier aircraft with more than 30 passenger seats were equipped with TCAS II.

Furthermore, FAA has recently proposed a new regulation to require certain cargo airlines to install TCAS to minimize the possibility of midair collisions. The proposed regulation would require affected aircraft to be equipped with TCAS II or another FAA-approved traffic alert and collision avoidance system no later than October 31, 2003.

---

[51]This applies to 14 C.F.R. 91 (general aviation), 14 C.F.R 121 (commercial airlines), and 14 C.F.R. 135 (aircraft with six or more passenger seats).

The Military Services Have Recently Begun Installation of GPWS and TCAS

The military services were aware of FAA's requirements for installing GPWS and TCAS on civil aircraft and have requested technical information from the agency on these technologies. While the military has lagged behind FAA in issuing similar mandates for its passenger- and troop-carrying aircraft, the Department of Defense (DOD) recently required each branch of the military to devise a plan for installing TCAS on its fleet of passenger-and troop-carrying aircraft. Soon after then-Secretary of Commerce Ronald Brown and 34 others were killed in April 1996 in an Air Force passenger-carrying aircraft that was equipped with GPWS, but not the enhanced version, the secretary of defense mandated a program to improve navigation and safety capabilities for passenger-and troop-carrying aircraft.

In August 1996, the Air Force published its Navigation and Safety Equipment Master Plan for DOD Passenger-Carrying Aircraft, which established guidance for equipping passenger-and troop-carrying aircraft, including GPWS and TCAS. The plan calls for two phases of implementation. Phase 1 requires installation by 2001 on all equipment used to transport senior military leaders, and Phase 2 requires installation by 2005 of all equipment components, including GPWS and TCAS, on remaining passenger-and troop-carrying aircraft.

In 1997, the DOD Defense Science Board Task Force on Aviation Safety found GPWS and TCAS to be effective in significantly reducing the risks of a major accident (e.g., fatal accidents or total loss of aircraft). The task force membership included a cross section of representation from the aviation community—the airlines, universities, military services, and FAA consultants. According to the board, GPWS and TCAS provide both safety and flight efficiency benefits and significant opportunities exist to leverage NASA, FAA, and commercial airline research and development initiatives pertaining to aviation safety.

In April 1998, the Office of the Secretary of Defense issued a memorandum to the secretaries of the Army, Navy, and Air Force to accelerate their installation of TCAS. The military services are now moving forward to implement this memorandum's requirements on the following schedules.

Army: No Army-specific policy directing field units to install GPWS or TCAS in aircraft exists. Rather, the Army relies on the April 1998 DOD memorandum as its prevailing guidance for TCAS. According to officials from the Department of the Army, as of August 2001, units had equipped 38 of the Army's 294 fixed wing aircraft with EGPWS and 90 of these same aircraft with TCAS. The remaining fixed wing aircraft must be equipped

with these technologies by fiscal year 2006. The Army has not equipped
any of its rotary wing aircraft (i.e., helicopters) with GPWS or TCAS and
currently has no plans to do so. According to an Army safety official, the
Army's helicopters are typically operated at very low altitudes and pilots
are generally able to make effective visual contact with any hilly or
mountainous terrain and take action to avoid contact with the terrain
without the assistance of GPWS. As such, the Army would rather dedicate
its limited resources to improving its visual guidance systems for these
aircraft. Furthermore, according to Army officials, Army helicopters are
equipped with "radar altimeter" in lieu of GPWS, with the exception of
some legacy aircraft that are being phased out of the fleet.

Navy: In December 1996, the Navy Air Board agreed that installing safety
technology (e.g., TCAS) into new and existing aircraft would improve
safety. In June 1998, the Navy implemented a new policy requiring
installation of TCAS and other safety equipment in newly produced and
"re-manufactured" aircraft.[52] In addition, it required passenger-and troop-
carrying aircraft to be equipped or retrofitted with additional commercial
safety systems that are already standard equipment in comparable civilian
aircraft.

Air Force: In 1996, the Air Force began installing TCAS in its passenger-
carrying aircraft and is moving forward to implement the DOD guidance
cited above.

Coast Guard: In 1998, the Coast Guard completed installation of TCAS in
its entire inventory of fixed wing and rotary-wing aircraft. In addition,
they have equipped their fleet of C-130 aircraft with GPWS. However, the
majority of the Coast Guard fleet is comprised of helicopters for which
GPWS technology is relatively new. According to a senior Coast Guard
safety official, due to the dynamic nature of rotorcraft flight as compared
to fixed wing aircraft flight,[53] making use of GPWS on helicopters is much
more difficult and has led technology development to lag behind that for
fixed wing aircraft. This official also said that the Coast Guard spends the
majority of its time flying over water and uses "radar altimeter" equipment

---

[52]Some aircraft are "re-manufactured" rather than being replaced. This involves
refurbishing aircraft to varying degrees to install updated parts and materials.

[53]Helicopters can stop, pedal turn, and hover, while fixed wing aircraft are often operated
in a fairly narrow band of forward motion, which makes their near-term flight path more
predictable.

to monitor the clearance under the aircraft along with a horn set by the
pilot to alert flight crews when a helicopter descends below an established
minimum altitude. In addition, this official noted that FAA has not
mandated the use of GPWS or its enhanced version in civil helicopters, but
that a certified enhanced GPWS became available last year and the Coast
Guard is monitoring the results of its use.

Appendix VI: Case Study on Flight Operational Quality Assurance (FOQA) Programs

Flight Operational Quality Assurance (FOQA) programs allow routine flight data to be collected and analyzed to detect and resolve potential safety, training, and maintenance issues. The experience of domestic and foreign airlines with these programs attests to their potential to enhance aviation safety. Given the potential of FOQA programs to improve both civil and military aviation safety, this case study was selected to determine the current status and pace of efforts by the Federal Aviation Administration (FAA), the aviation industry, and the military services to put them in place.

History of FOQA

In its 1992 study for FAA, the Flight Safety Foundation coined the term "Flight Operational Quality Assurance Program" and defined it as "a program for obtaining and analyzing data recorded in flight to improve flight crew performance, air carrier training programs and operating procedures, air traffic control procedures, airport maintenance and design, and aircraft operations and design."[54] The objective of a FOQA program is to use flight data to detect technical flaws, unsafe practices, or conditions outside of desired operating procedures early enough to allow timely intervention to avert accidents or incidents. For example, FOQA data can be used to improve aviation safety by identifying hazardous approaches into a particular airport and helping to justify to FAA the need for a new approach pattern that is less likely to lead to an accident under adverse conditions, or to improve pilot training. These data can also yield operational efficiencies, such as identifying and mitigating flight practices that place unnecessary strain on aircraft engines and other parts.

Modern commercial aircraft contain sophisticated electronic systems that gather, process, and manage digital data on many aspects of flight. These data originate from various systems and sensors throughout the aircraft. Some of these data are continuously recorded by the aircraft's digital flight data recorder to help investigators understand what happened if the aircraft is involved in an accident or a serious incident.[55] Designed to

---

[54]*Air Carrier Voluntary Flight Operational Quality Assurance Program*, Flight Safety Foundation (1992).

[55]The National Transportation Safety Board (NTSB), the official source of information on airline accidents, defines accidents as events in which individuals are killed or suffer serious injury, or the aircraft is substantially damaged. Incidents are defined as occurrences other than accidents associated with the operation of an aircraft that affect or could affect the safety of operations (49 C.F.R. 830.2). In the military, Class A Mishaps are accidents and Class B and C Mishaps are serious incidents.

survive crashes, flight data recorders generally retain the data recorded during the last 25 hours of flight. Airlines with FOQA programs typically use a device called a quick access recorder to capture flight data onto a removable optical disk that facilitates the data's frequent removal from the aircraft.[56]

British Airways has had a FOQA-type program in place since the late 1960s. This program has served as the model for similar programs in the United States and around the world. In July 1995, as part of FAA's strategy to achieve significant reductions in aviation accident rates—despite the rapid increase in air travel anticipated over the next decade—the agency initiated a three-year, $5.5 million FOQA Demonstration Project to promote the voluntary implementation of FOQA programs by U.S. airlines. The project was designed to facilitate the start-up of voluntary airline FOQA programs and to assess the costs, benefits, and safety enhancements associated with such programs. FAA provided hardware and software to United, US Airways, and Continental and each has implemented FOQA programs according to the demonstration project requirements. Since that time, others including Delta Airlines and American Airlines, have also initiated FOQA programs. The rules under the project required airlines to provide FAA with access to "aggregate" FOQA data on the airlines' premises and did not require them to submit these data to FAA. See table 2 for a timeline of key events pertaining to the implementation of FOQA programs.

Table 2: Flight Operational Quality Assurance Programs Timeline

Date	Agency, industry, or military branch	Action
Late 1960s	British Airways	Inaugurates first airline FOQA program.
1992	Flight Safety Foundation	Publishes study recognizing that acceptance of FOQA programs by the aviation industry hinges on adequate protection of data collected.
March 1993	FAA	Begins rulemaking effort. However, progress quickly stalled by airline concerns about FAA's intended use of FOQA data.

---

[56]These data typically include the parameters required to be collected on the aircraft's flight data recorder plus many more parameters.

Date	Agency, industry, or military branch	Action
July 1995	FAA	Begins a FOQA demonstration project—"Demoproj"— and issues statement indicating commitment to using FOQA data for safety analysis purposes only.
1997	Department of Justice (DOJ)	Cautioned FAA that a federal regulator may not be able to exempt regulated parties from enforcement actions, even if information is submitted voluntarily.
1997 – 2000	FAA and DOJ	Work together to develop a proposed FOQA rule that would be acceptable to all stakeholders (e.g., industry, FAA, and DOJ).
November 1997	Defense Science Board	Publishes report finding that inconsistencies exist between civil aviation's commitment to use FOQA programs for safety purposes and the military services' own such commitment. Issues two related recommendations to military.
1998	FAA	Publishes a policy statement indicating an intent to use FOQA data for enforcement purposes, but only when rule violations are "egregious" (i.e., criminal or negligent).
October 1999	Joint service safety chiefs (heads of the military services' safety centers)	Agree informally that FOQA has value and endorse projects and research by all military services.
July 2000	FAA	Formally publishes a Notice of Proposed Rulemaking on voluntary implementation of FOQA programs by U.S. airlines.
August 2000	Joint service safety chiefs	Formally endorse military FOQA programs—"MFOQA"— and recommend full funding for their implementation.
July 2001	FAA	Rule issued protecting voluntarily submitted aviation safety and security data are protected from release (e.g., under Freedom of Information Act).
October 2001	FAA and DOT	Publication of final FOQA rule.

Source: FAA, airlines, and the military services.

FAA Continues to Encourage FOQA Programs Among Airlines

FAA efforts to encourage the implementation of FOQA programs have been under way for nearly a decade. In addition to the FOQA demonstration project mentioned earlier, FAA has issued separate rules on FOQA and issued a rule to protect those submitting voluntary aviation safety information.

FAA Has Taken Steps to Alleviate Aviation Industry Concerns About Data Use

Key aviation industry stakeholders, including airline executives, pilots and other crewmembers, are enthusiastic about FOQA's continuing potential for saving lives, but they are nevertheless concerned about the possible consequences of a FAA rule about FOQA. These stakeholders considered the draft rule to be overly intrusive because of the agency's insistence that these data be removed from airlines' property and concerns about how these data will be used (e.g., to take enforcement actions against pilots or airlines). However, as requested by industry, the final rule limits the use of FOQA data by FAA to enforcement actions for criminal and deliberate acts.

The 1992 Flight Safety Foundation study recognized that the acceptance of FOQA programs by the aviation industry hinges on adequate protection of the data collected. In particular, the study noted that airlines were concerned about increased accident liability and possible punitive actions by FAA, for rule infractions that could be revealed by FOQA. Airlines are also concerned about the release of these data to the media and the potential for unfair criticism of their commitment to safety if data are not interpreted in the proper context. Pilots' concerns focused on possible punitive actions by airline management and FAA. We have also reported that resolution of data protection issues was the primary impediment to the implementation of FOQA programs among the major domestic carriers.[57]

FAA began its FOQA rulemaking effort in January 1993. However, progress on this rulemaking stalled due to unresolved concerns among the airline industry about whether or not FAA would use the data submitted voluntarily by the airlines under FOQA to take enforcement action. Before initiating the FOQA Demonstration Project in 1995, FAA issued a statement that it was committed to not using FOQA data for enforcement purposes. FAA reiterated this position in 1998.

According to FAA officials, when the agency reestablished the FOQA rulemaking effort in 1997, it encountered some resistance from DOJ. Specifically, DOJ raised concerns that a government regulatory agency such as FAA may not be able to exempt those who are regulated from enforcement actions based on information received from them, voluntary or not. Between December 1997 and June 2000, rulemaking officials, in conjunction with the DOJ, worked to develop a rule that was acceptable to the industry and the administrator. However, in response to continued industry concerns about the use of FOQA data for enforcement, the FAA administrator published in 1998 a policy statement that the agency would only use FOQA data for enforcement purposes in egregious cases (e.g., if the violation were deliberate, involved a criminal offense, or the violator

---

[57]*Aviation Safety: Efforts to Implement Flight Operational Quality Assurance Programs* (RCED-98-10, Dec. 2, 1997).

had committed a similar violation within the previous five years). The statement further asserted that, in order to qualify for protection from punitive action based on analysis of FOQA data, an airline must submit to FAA for approval a FOQA implementation and operation plan describing its procedures for taking remedial action on any identified deficiencies that become apparent as the result of FOQA data analysis.

FAA Has Finalized FOQA Rule

In October 2001, FAA published a final rule on FOQA encouraging voluntary implementation of FOQA programs by airlines. The final rule provided that information obtained from airlines' voluntary FOQA programs could be used in enforcement actions against air carriers, commercial operators, or airmen (e.g., pilots), only for criminal or deliberate acts. The final rule requires air carriers participating in FOQA programs to submit aggregate data to FAA for use in monitoring safety trends. FAA could also use these aggregated data as a basis for initiating safety rulemakings.[58]

However, there are outstanding concerns within the aviation industry about the rule's possible ramifications. For example, the final rule says that FAA will maintain the discretion to take enforcement action and that this action will not be affected by the final rule. Concerns also persist about the removal of FOQA data from airlines' premises because this makes the airlines vulnerable to other federal agencies' reviews of the data. FAA's definition of "aggregate data" is also unclear; if it refers to a single airline's aggregate data, this is not acceptable to the airline industry, while aggregate data reported industrywide would be acceptable.

FAA Issues Rule Intended to Protect Safety Data That Are Voluntarily Submitted From Release to the Public

In June 2001, FAA issued a rule[59] that protects voluntarily submitted aviation safety and security data from release, for example, under the Freedom of Information Act. With this type of protection in place, the agency is confident that it will be able to obtain more voluntarily submitted safety and security data than it does currently. However, some aviation industry stakeholders told us that they are still reluctant to submit such data—fearing that the media and/or the public will misinterpret it.

---

[58]Airlines submit data to FAA, which determines if these data are "voluntary." For example, any data generated as part of a compliance requirement *must* be given to FAA.

[59]The Federal Aviation Reauthorization Act of 1996 requires FAA to protect aviation safety and security information that is submitted voluntarily (49 U.S.C. 40123).

Another rule offering limited protection for voluntarily submitted FOQA data is pending.

The U.S. Military Services Are Still in the Early Stages of Developing FOQA Programs

The U.S. military services readily acknowledge the potential benefits of implementing FOQA programs despite varied mission requirements that could make implementing such programs more difficult for them than it has been for commercial aviation.[60] To date, the military services have taken various levels of action—from high-level discussions about how to proceed with FOQA to initiating demonstration projects for specific aircraft types.

In February 1997, a Defense Science Board (DSB) report "Task Force Report on Aviation Safety," conducted at the request of the Congress, found that "inconsistencies exist between aircraft used for passenger and troop transport and civil aircraft leased for similar purposes" and made two recommendations specifically related to FOQA. First, it recommended that a policy be developed for military transport aircraft that requires the same safety equipment (flight data recorders) as that required for commercial airlines—with waivers to be approved only at the service chief level.[61] It also recommended that the military services "fully exploit the new opportunities afforded by flight data recorders to collect performance and hardware maintenance data," and noted the value of flight data to monitoring aircraft conditions, crew performance and communication, and aircraft maintenance.

In October 1999, the Joint Service Safety Chiefs (JSSC) agreed that FOQA had value and endorsed projects and research by all services. A Memorandum of Agreement signed by the JSSC on August 28, 2000, formally endorsed military FOQA and recommended full funding of required resources. In response to the safety chiefs' endorsement of FOQA and in an effort to increase cross-service communication on the subject, the military has held two FOQA conferences and plans to hold such meetings annually for the combined services. The first conference, held in

---

[60]Airlines have the advantage of analyzing FOQA data from aircraft that typically "fly very prescribed procedures from point A to point B." In contrast, military aircraft are operated using a wide range of maneuvers that vary by aircraft type and mission, while comparable maneuvers are simply not done in civil aircraft. As a result, the military may find it more difficult to analyze FOQA data.

[61]Each of the military services has a safety chief responsible for overseeing safety issues, including aviation.

October 2000, introduced the services to FOQA; the second conference
(held in March 2001) emphasized economics, policy, technology, and
analysis associated with FOQA. Aside from the safety chiefs' formal
endorsement of FOQA and the two related conferences, the military
branches have taken only initial steps in implementing formalized FOQA
programs, due in part to budget tradeoffs between aircraft safety and other
mission-readiness needs. See table 3 for the status of the military services'
efforts to implement FOQA programs.

Table 3: Status of Military Efforts to Implement FOQA Programs as of August 1, 2001

Authority	Key actions
Air Force	Policy established the Aircraft Information Program with a main goal of enabling FOQA (February 2001). Selected a software contractor to support a one-year FOQA demonstration project (June 2001). Has collected data since 1994 on nearly 11,000 flights. The software support obtained in June 2001 has allowed them to start processing these data. They will use a maximum of 30 C-17 aircraft at McChord Air Force Base in Washington state to operate this demonstration.
Marine Corps	The Executive Safety Board set a goal to "initiate the FOQA process with the MV-22," the Marine's newest airplane (August 2000). It also set a secondary goal to "expand the FOQA process to other aircraft with digital electronic systems, as soon as possible."
Navy	Has "proven" the value of the FOQA concept using the C-2 aircraft. Is still debating whether FOQA should be used as a training tool to improve aviation safety or as an enforcement tool to protect taxpayer investments in naval aircraft. According to a senior Navy Safety Center official, the Navy could improve its mission effectiveness by implementing a military FOQA program to improve pilot training, make better use of limited flight hours, and ultimately train better pilots. However, implementing FOQA in the Navy would be a "tough sell" given the basic needs competing for resources, such as funding to repair aircraft engines.
Coast Guard	Currently examining how best to establish a FOQA program. All helicopters are equipped with Flight Data Recorders (FDR). A proposal to equip Falcon and C-130 fixed wing aircraft has been submitted within the Coast Guard; however, the Falcon aircraft are old, expensive to equip, and may be nearing the end of their service lives.
Army	Is drafting and staffing a military FOQA usage policy that mirrors FAA's protection of FOQA data. In addition, some aircraft are already equipped with the hardware necessary for collecting FOQA data. Furthermore, some aircraft have been/are continuing to be equipped with FDRs or new digital technology to capture flight data.

Source: Military services.

Appendix VII: Case Study on Communication Delays Between the Air Force and Civil Aviation Community

During the National Transportation Safety Board (NTSB) accident investigation into the July 1996 crash of TWA Flight 800, it was discovered that the Air Force had experienced problems with overheating in the center wing fuel tank of the E4-B aircraft (a military variant of the 747). In response, the Air Force contracted with Boeing's Military Group to study the problem between 1979 and 1980; the group issued a report to the Air Force in 1980. However, the report was not shared with the civil aviation officials until 1999.[62] This case study illustrates the importance of effective and timely communication between the military and civilian aviation communities on similar aviation safety problems.

The Air Force was concerned about the E-4B engines continuing to run satisfactorily if a main (wing) tank fuel pump malfunctioned. In addition, there was concern over the running of the air conditioning packs under the center wing tank for extended periods of time when the airplane was on alert, idling on the ground with engines running for 48 hours. In this mode, the center wing tank was full of fuel, and heated up slowly to a high temperature. The 1980 Air Force report prepared by Boeing's Military Group found that, under certain circumstances, air conditioning wires running through the fuel tank could create a potential safety problem, but determined that the engine would continue to operate successfully provided certain operating restrictions were implemented.

The central focus of the Air Force's concerns and Boeing's analysis was fuel pump performance, not fuel tank flammability. Federal Aviation Administration (FAA) officials said that this test was not envisioned as one of flammability of the vapor in the fuel tank, but merely to assess the effectiveness of fuel being fed to the engine. They added that it was always assumed that fuel vapor might be flammable under certain conditions.[63] However, NTSB officials maintain that the information contained in this report would have assisted them with their accident investigations related

---

[62]*Transportation Safety: Information Concerning Why a 1980 Aircraft Report Was Not Provided Earlier to the National Transportation Safety Board* (GAO/OSI-00-2R, Nov. 3, 1999).

[63]According to FAA, the philosophy at the time and until shortly after the TWA Flight 800 accident was that no ignition sources be allowed inside of fuel tanks. It was not until August 1996 that a Boeing 747 flight test was conducted to investigate what effect the center tank heating would have on fuel vapor flammability. FAA was aware that aircraft operated with the fuel tank in the flammability range under certain conditions. This is why FAA regulations require the elimination of ignition sources. However, NTSB has recommended a different approach to the problem; namely "inerting" the fuel so that it would not explode even if it came into contact with an ignited source.

to fuel tank flammability. While the report's authors did not recommend structural changes to the E-4B aircraft, they did recommended taking mitigating actions, such as flying the aircraft with the center fuel tank empty.

In July 1996, NTSB began its investigation into the crash of TWA Flight 800. As part of the investigation, Boeing was requested to search its database for any information concerning heating problems with the 747's center (wing) fuel tanks. According to both NTSB and Boeing officials, the Boeing Commercial Airplane Group told NTSB that it had no such data. However, in December 1997, the Air Force report came to the attention of the Boeing Military Group when it was found during a "housecleaning effort." It was determined that the report was the property of the Air Force and subsequently sent to the Air Force Oklahoma City Air Logistics Command (OC-ALC).

Boeing officials told us that the report should have been located and turned over to NTSB in 1996, even though the Boeing Military Group prepared it for the Air Force. They stated that human error had caused an incomplete search to be made of the Boeing records system for information on heat studies involving center (wing) fuel tanks. A senior Boeing safety official told us that the company has modified its electronic library to allow key word searches across all of the company's reports. Its accident investigation processes have also been revised to include electronic searches for technical documents.

In 1998, the Air Force OC-ALC initiated an Independent Review Team (IRT) to discuss center (wing) fuel tank issues connected with the E-4B aircraft in light of recommendations issued by the NTSB following its investigation of the TWA Flight 800 accident. The Air Force OC-ALC held an IRT meeting in March 1999 to continue to review safety issues concerning the center (wing) fuel tank of the E-4B aircraft. As part of that meeting, the Air Force included the report on the meeting agenda. Air Force officials told us that the report was put on the agenda to show that the E-4B aircraft was equipped somewhat differently and was capable of operating under more difficult conditions than the commercial 747, not for safety reasons. Participants in this meeting included officials from Boeing's Commercial Airplane Group and Military Group and NTSB. Officials of both Boeing's Commercial Airplane Group and NTSB told us that this was the first time they had heard about the report.

Air Force OC-ALC officials told us that when Boeing brought the report to their attention, it was placed on the IRT agenda for discussion. These officials said that they did not intentionally withhold the report from the NTSB because both military and civilian personnel in their organization considered it to be an operational or readiness study, not a safety study. The NTSB director told us that, after the March 1999 IRT meeting, NTSB requested a copy of the entire study from the Air Force, but instead received a summary. In June, after intervention by a U.S. Senate committee,[64] the Air Force provided the entire study to NTSB.

A senior NTSB official told us that it is not likely that earlier sharing of the report's findings would have prevented the crash of TWA Flight 800. However, had NTSB received the study in 1996 following the crash of TWA Flight 800, it would have saved valuable time and resources in conducting its investigation. Both the NTSB's chairman and director of aviation noted that the study might have been very helpful to the NTSB in its 1990 investigation of a Boeing 737 aircraft explosion at Manila Airport in the Philippines—the explosion occurred in the aircraft's center fuel tank. According to both officials, it is possible that, if they had received the Boeing study by 1990, safety recommendations made as a result of the TWA Flight 800 crash could have been issued sooner.

In August 2000, NTSB released its report on the TWA Flight 800 accident, which included the following statement regarding the report Boeing prepared for the Air Force on fuel tank overheating in the E4-B:

The Safety Board recognizes that the military variant of the 747 is not directly comparable to the civilian 747 and that the focus of that study was fuel pump functionality, not flammability. Nonetheless, it is unfortunate that potentially relevant information about 747 center wing [fuel] tank overheating and corrective measures were not provided to the FAA or to 747 operators earlier.

---

[64]Subcommittee on Administrative Oversight and the Courts, Committee on the Judiciary, U.S. Senate.

Appendix VIII: Case Study on Strandflex Control Cable

In January 1999, a former employee of the Strandflex Company alleged in federal court that the corporation was not conducting quality assurance tests to ensure that its wire rope used in the assembly of aircraft control cables met military specifications. According to the Department of Defense (DOD), this wire rope is critical to the safe operation of flight control systems (e.g., aircraft rudders, wing flaps, brakes, and steering) on affected aircraft. However, Federal Aviation Administration (FAA) officials contend that this wire rope is not always critical to flight safety because civil federal aviation regulations require that aircraft control systems incorporate redundancies, meaning that failure of control cables would not cause loss of the airplane.[65]

In response to the allegation against the Strandflex Company, the Defense Criminal Investigative Service initiated an investigation and an independent test by DOD demonstrated the wire rope did not consistently meet strength requirements. The Department of Defense Office of Inspector General (DODIG) alerted the military services and FAA concurrently in May 1999. The military services took prompt action to notify responsible officials to assess the extent of safety hazards and correct them. FAA took just over a year to notify the civil aviation community. FAA officials acknowledged that there was a delay, but said that they had assessed the situation and concluded that it did not require urgent action. However, the agency's inaction resulted in a Department of Transportation Office of Inspector General (DOTIG) investigation into the delay and FAA's overall process for issuing notifications of unapproved parts. On May 30, 2001, the Strandflex Company admitted to making false claims to the United States and falsely certifying that its aircraft control cable wire rope met U.S. military specifications and was ordered by a U.S. District Court judge to pay a criminal fine and restitution.

DOTIG Has Reported That FAA Delayed Action on Strandflex Concerns

Concerned about FAA's delay in notifying air carriers of possible problems with Strandflex cables, a June 2000 Congressional request called for the DOTIG to investigate, among other things, the timeliness and effectiveness of FAA's response to information about possible flaws in the Strandflex control cable.

---

[65]FAA officials also told us that civil aircraft cable assemblies are often designed to be five times stronger than they need to be. Furthermore, once aircraft control cables are assembled, they are tested in a manner that would reveal weaknesses in the wire rope.

In March 2001, the DOTIG reported that FAA did not act in a timely manner in response to the information it received about Strandflex, confirming that just over a year had passed between the time that the DODIG notified FAA about possible problems with Strandflex and the date that FAA published an Unapproved Parts Notification (UPN) on Strandflex. A UPN disseminates information about unapproved parts to the civil aviation community.[66]

Furthermore, the DOTIG identified three primary factors that accounted for FAA's untimely response: FAA (1) misfiled the initial notification, resulting in an initial delay of approximately 3 months; (2) spent an additional month forwarding a Suspect Unapproved Parts investigative request to the New England Regional office for further investigation; (3) delayed an additional 4 months because a legal challenge made it reluctant to issue advisory field notifications about suspect unapproved parts.[67]

FAA Has Taken Action to Improve Communication with DOD in Response to the DOTIG Investigation of Strandflex

FAA notified the DODIG in August 2000 of the need for DOD to send alert messages pertaining to suspect unapproved parts directly to FAA's Suspect Unapproved Parts Program Office. This action was taken in response to the DOTIG's investigation of FAA's delay in alerting the civil aviation community about potential quality assurance problems with Strandflex wire rope. Specifically, DOD alerts about suspect unapproved parts were being sent to FAA's Civil Aviation Security Office[68] rather than FAA's Suspect Unapproved Parts Program Office. While the DOTIG did not identify this as a key contributor to the year-long delay by FAA, such simple communication breakdowns as not sending safety notifications to all responsible officials could lead to delays in addressing potential hazards. In its response to the DOTIG finding of weaknesses in FAA's

---

[66]*OIG Investigation of Responses to Information About a Serious Flaw in Aircraft Cables*, U.S. Department of Transportation, Office of the Inspector General (Mar. 2, 2001, Report Number CC-2000-290).

[67]FAA attributed its reluctance to a September 1999 challenge from an attorney representing members of the aviation community regarding the agency's authority to issue such notifications. The attorney cited concerns that field notifications are purely advisory in nature, that no corrective action is mandatory, and that the companies named in field notifications are not afforded the opportunity to respond to the issues—violating their due process rights.

[68]FAA's Office of Civil Aviation Security, Internal Security Investigation Program, often provides investigative services at the request of other FAA organizational units on a wide range of subjects, including unapproved aircraft parts.

overall processing of UPNs, the FAA manager for the Suspect Unapproved Parts Program Office advised the DOTIG that corrective action had been taken to ensure that all DOD alert messages were now sent directly to FAA's Suspect Unapproved Part Program Office. According to FAA and DOD officials, while FAA's Office of Civil Aviation Security remains the addressee in the official letter from DOD alerting FAA to potential problems with suspect unapproved parts, the FAA Unapproved Parts Program Office is included on DOD's list of facsimile recipients and receives notifications immediately after signature.

OFFICE OF THE UNDER SECRETARY OF DEFENSE

3000 DEFENSE PENTAGON
WASHINGTON, DC 20301-3000

ACQUISITION,
TECHNOLOGY
AND LOGISTICS

JAN. 1 4 2002

Mr. Peter Guerrero
Director, Physical Infrastructure Issues
U.S. General Accounting Office
441 G Street, NW
Washington, DC 20548

Dear Mr. Guerrero:

This is the Department of Defense (DoD) response to the GAO draft report, "AVIATION SAFETY: FAA and DoD Communication and Response to Similar Safety Concerns," dated November 30, 2001 (GAO Code 395001/GAO-02-77).

DoD agrees with the report and has the attached comments.

Thank you for the opportunity to review the final draft report. Like the Federal Aviation Administration, we are most concerned about aviation safety and look forward to a closer working relationship.

My action officer is Mr. Craig Schilder, who can be reached at (703) 604-1612 or craig.schilder@osd.mil if you have any questions.

Sincerely,

Raymond F. DuBois, Jr.
Deputy Under Secretary of Defense
(Installations and Environment)

Attachments:
As stated

**GAO DRAFT REPORT – DATED NOVEMBER 30, 2001
GAO CODE 395001/GAO-02-77**

**"AVIATION SAFETY: FAA AND DOD COMMUNICATION AND
RESPONSE TO SIMILAR SAFETY CONCERNS"**

DEPARTMENT OF DEFENSE TECHNICAL COMMENTS

1. Page 3, paragraph 1, line 9 and page 11, paragraph 1. Replace: "…five aviation safety positions were abolished" with "…five safety positions were abolished." Reason: OSD did not have 5 safety positions that were dedicated to only aviation safety. In fact the aviation safety responsibilities were shared by all.

2. Page 36: Paragraph 2, line 2, Replace "factual and privileged" with (safety investigation reports) contain two types of information "nonprivileged" and "privileged". Reason: Proper identification of the report data.

3. Page 40, Replace the first two sentences under the heading of United States Air Force. Delete: According to an Air Force wiring expert, the Air Force <u>did not experience</u> any problems with aromatic polyimide but were aware of the concerns raised by the Navy and Coast Guard. It sponsored the development of new wire insulation, the TKT Composite (Telfon-Kapton-Teflon) manufactured by DuPont, that eliminated problems exhibited by aromatic polyimide alone.

Page 40, Insert: According to an Air Force wiring expert, the Air Force <u>also experienced</u> failures associated with aromatic polyimide wiring and took steps to mitigate failures. It was also aware of the concerns raised by the Navy and sponsored a research program that led to the development of a composite wiring construction (Teflon/Kapton/Teflon) that mitigated many of the problems exhibited by aromatic polyimide.

Reason: Air Force requested clarification.

**GAO DRAFT REPORT – DATED NOVEMBER 30, 2001
GAO CODE 395001/GAO-02-77**

**"AVIATION SAFETY: FAA AND DOD COMMUNICATION AND
RESPONSE TO SIMILAR SAFETY CONCERNS"**

**DEPARTMENT OF DEFENSE COMMENTS
TO THE RECOMMENDATION**

RECOMMENDATION: The GAO recommended that the Secretary of Defense
develop a memorandum of agreement (MOA) with the Administrator of the Federal
Aviation Administration. The MOA would ensure the systematic exchange of critical
safety information. The MOA should define the types of safety information to be
exchanged, the mechanisms for exchanging this information, and the parties responsible
for this exchange. The MOA should also establish a mechanism for the two departments
to exchange information on how they have responded to specific safety concerns. (Page
23/GAO Draft Report)

DOD RESPONSE:

We agree that a memorandum of agreement with the Federal Aviation Administration
(FAA) would enhance the exchange of critical information, even though several Navy
and Air Force organizations frequently hold meetings with the FAA. Also, we have two
directives that require exchange of critical aviation safety information.

Appendix X: GAO Contacts and Staff Acknowledgments

GAO Contacts

Peter F. Guerrero (202) 512-2834

Acknowledgments

In addition to the individual named above, Aaron Casey, Beverly Dulaney, Colin Fallon, David Hooper, Maren McAvoy, Sara-Ann Moessbauer, Robert White, and Mario Zavala made key contributions to this report.

GAO's Mission	The General Accounting Office, the investigative arm of Congress, exists to support Congress in meeting its constitutional responsibilities and to help improve the performance and accountability of the federal government for the American people. GAO examines the use of public funds; evaluates federal programs and policies; and provides analyses, recommendations, and other assistance to help Congress make informed oversight, policy, and funding decisions. GAO's commitment to good government is reflected in its core values of accountability, integrity, and reliability.
Obtaining Copies of GAO Reports and Testimony	The fastest and easiest way to obtain copies of GAO documents is through the Internet. GAO's Web site (www.gao.gov) contains abstracts and full-text files of current reports and testimony and an expanding archive of older products. The Web site features a search engine to help you locate documents using key words and phrases. You can print these documents in their entirety, including charts and other graphics.

Each day, GAO issues a list of newly released reports, testimony, and correspondence. GAO posts this list, known as "Today's Reports," on its Web site daily. The list contains links to the full-text document files. To have GAO e-mail this list to you every afternoon, go to www.gao.gov and select "Subscribe to daily e-mail alert for newly released products" under the GAO Reports heading. |
| Order by Mail or Phone | The first copy of each printed report is free. Additional copies are $2 each. A check or money order should be made out to the Superintendent of Documents. GAO also accepts VISA and Mastercard. Orders for 100 or more copies mailed to a single address are discounted 25 percent. Orders should be sent to:

U.S. General Accounting Office
P.O. Box 37050
Washington, D.C. 20013

To order by Phone: Voice: (202) 512-6000
                            TDD: (202) 512-2537
                            Fax: (202) 512-6061 |
| Visit GAO's Document Distribution Center | GAO Building
Room 1100, 700 4th Street, NW (corner of 4th and G Streets, NW)
Washington, D.C. 20013 |
| To Report Fraud, Waste, and Abuse in Federal Programs | Contact:

Web site: www.gao.gov/fraudnet/fraudnet.htm,
E-mail: fraudnet@gao.gov, or
1-800-424-5454 or (202) 512-7470 (automated answering system). |
| Public Affairs | Jeff Nelligan, Managing Director, NelliganJ@gao.gov (202) 512-4800
U.S. General Accounting Office, 441 G. Street NW, Room 7149,
Washington, D.C. 20548 |